UNEXPECTED PLEASURES

Leaving heterosexuality for a lesbian life

TAMSIN WILTON

First published 2002 by Diva Books,
an imprint of Millivres Prowler Ltd, part of the Millivres Prowler Group,
Spectrum House, 32-34 Gordon House Road, London NW5 1LP, UK

A CIP catalogue record for this book is available from the British Library.

ISBN 1-873741-72-3

Distributed in the UK and Europe by Airlift Book Company,
8 The Arena, Mollison Avenue, Enfield, Middlesex, EN3 7NJ, UK
Tel: 020 8804 0400
Distributed in North America by Consortium Book Sales and Distribution,
1045 Westgate Drive, Saint Paul, MN 55114-1065, USA
Tel: 651 221 9035 / 800 283 3572
Distributed in Australia by Bulldog Books, PO Box 700, Beaconsfield, NSW 2014

Printed and bound in the EU by WS Bookwell, Juva, Finland

This book is dedicated to my staunch friend Hilary – 18 years of friendship and counting – and, with great respect and gratitude, to all the women who shared their stories with me. To each one of you: I will never forget your strength and honesty, and I wish you godspeed on your heart's journey.

Contents

Acknowledgements

This research was funded by a fellowship from the Faculty of Health and Social Care at the University of the West of England at Bristol. Thanks to my advisory team, Robin Means, Peter Hampson, Steph Keeble and Steve West.

When I told my friends I was working on another book, reaction was unanimous. "You're not going to turn into *that* person again, are you?" I know I am extremely difficult to live with when I am writing, and for putting up with this I have to thank Hilary Lindsay, Steph Keeble, Lesley Doyal, Lynne Walker, Jacky Brine, Debbie Epstein, Rebecca Boden, my gorgeous son Tom Coveney and my dear daughter-out-law, Stephie. For support of various kinds I thank Hilary Bright (for putting my arms back together), Lyn Jennings, Guy Marshall (whose mail box was overused), Kim Hastings, Carly Hall, the lovely Elaine at the Glass Bar, Netty and her anonymous friend (you know who you are!) and the members of the Sexuality Research Interest Group. Hazel Bunting, Diane Mayo and Leigh Taylor womanfully transcribed the tapes and Tony Rigby returned from the distant past to argue me out of my certainties. Helen de Pinho, Nicki, Annie, Funeka and all the fabulous queers from the Triangle Project in Cape Town get big kisses for welcoming and helping me in a strange land, and the Lesbian Study Group of the British Sociological Association get hugs for keeping me sane(ish). Finally, thanks to Helen and the team at Diva for making sure that this gets out where it belongs.

Introduction

QUESTIONS AND MORE QUESTIONS

This book is the result of over three years' hard work tracking down and talking with women who, at some point in their lives, left heterosexuality behind for the love of women. As any social scientist will tell you, lesbians are a famously 'hard to reach' group who, for very good reasons, are not inclined to trust academic researchers with information about their lives and loves. This was not my experience (I wish it was half as easy to find a lover!). I found them as far afield as Cape Town and as close to home as half a mile down the road. I met some in cafés and museums, interviewed others over the telephone, communicated via email with several in distant lands and whisked others away in the middle of conferences or social events. Many invited me into their homes and were as generous with cups of tea and pieces of home-made cake as they were with their time. Their stories form the heart of this book, in more ways than one.

It was an extraordinary three years, and left me with a store of fond memories and an immense respect for our resilience and willingness to take risks. But there was a serious purpose behind it all. I was searching for answers to questions which had dogged me, as an academic and as a lesbian, for years. I came out at the ripe old age of 35, having been quite happily and productively heterosexual up to that point. The tired old line "You just haven't met the right man yet" doesn't cut much ice with me; I have met several, thank you very much. And *still* I prefer women. Why? How long have you got?

I have never quite been able to find the right language to explain this process. Say "When I came out..." and people assume you must have been a lesbian all along and just took a while to work it out for yourself. Or they think you led a life of torment, hiding your true self beneath a heterosexual facade. Neither of these is true about me, although, as I was to discover, these things can and do happen.

On the other hand, if I say, "When I became a lesbian..." people look at me very strangely. Then the worried questions begin. How can anyone *become* a lesbian? Isn't it something you're born with or, at the very least, something caused by early childhood experiences? Haven't they found the gay gene now? The idea that I am claiming to have changed sexual orientation well into adult life seems threatening to most people, and tends to make them very anxious. After all, if sexuality is *not* fixed early on in life, who knows what might happen? Any woman might wake up one morning and – powee – find she's gone gay overnight.

Faced with some very anxious friends and colleagues, I had to admit that I was not too sure what had happened myself. After all, our sexuality feels very deep-rooted. How can it change so dramatically? And it wasn't only my straight friends who were anxious. My lesbian friends, too, found it difficult to cope with the notion that I used to be heterosexual. It was particularly difficult for them to hear that I had enjoyed being heterosexual and hadn't found sex with men disgusting or boring. Perhaps they were anxious about the possibility that I might wake up one morning and find myself consumed with a desire for men again. Many of them thought I was probably bisexual and in denial.

What happened to me certainly makes no sense in terms of most 'scientific' theories of sexuality. Put simply, I used to look at some men with pleasure and desire and I had great fun in bed with them. My male partners generally fell into the category of 'nice person' (though there were a few selfish bastards, of course), and were mostly willing and able to try out various ways of building an equal relationship. Yet by the time I hit 35 I couldn't imagine ever wanting sex with a man again, let alone an intimate relationship. So what happened? Did something in me just get worn out or used up? Was the 'lesbian' me the 'real' me all along? Or did I – and this is certainly what it feels like to me – just grow out of men and move on to the more adult pleasures of lesbian life?

As a human being, I wanted to be able to understand all this well enough to be able to explain it to my friends. As an academic, I was also puzzled by the claims made about sexual orientation by biological scientists. I have never been able to understand the fuss which greeted theories about a 'gay gene' or gay brain structure, let alone more obviously dotty claims about lesbians having longer or shorter fingers than straight women or having a distinctive inner-ear structure (both of these were perfectly serious claims made by perfectly serious scientists).

First, it baffled me that anyone would think these findings were credible, since it was so easy to drive a horse and cart through the experimental methods used by the researchers. Second, I couldn't accept the proposition that sexual orientation was somehow hard-wired into our biology, since this seems such a laughably weak explanation for the complexity of everyone's sexual desires and preferences. It seems likely that people *really* want to believe that their desires are programmed into them from birth, which has the advantage of letting them off the hook, as they don't have to defend any unpopular or socially unacceptable choices. But why should so many of us feel we need that kind of escape clause?

By setting out to explore the experiences of women who, like me, had found their sexual orientation *shifting* during the course of adulthood, I hoped to do two things. Firstly, to make sense of desire on a personal level and secondly, to provide some scientifically rigorous empirical evidence which would prove that biology simply *cannot* explain sexual attraction. I am hoping that all the neurobiologists, endocrinologists, finger-measurers and hearing-testers will flick through my evidence, realise the error of their ways and turn their attention to something more important, like finding a cure for HIV or mending the hole in the ozone layer. Of course they won't, because scientists don't read very widely. If they did, they would have stopped trying to find the cause of homosexuality decades ago. Sexual behaviour differs so dramatically between cultures, and can shift so rapidly between generations that any anthropologist or historian could have told them they were wasting their time. Perhaps they should unstick their eyes from the scanning electron microscope and get out more.

How these stories came to be told

This is not intended to be an academic book, so I am not going to bore you with lengthy accounts of my methodology. If you are interested, you will be able to read the full account (together with a more theoretical analysis of the interviews) in the other work I am going to write about the same project for an academic audience. However, in order to make sense of the stories which follow, it helps to have some idea of how they came to be told.

I was able to do the project because I won a research fellowship awarded by the Faculty of Health and Social Care at the University of the West of England in Bristol. I had been based in the faculty for many years, teaching sociology to nurses, midwives and social workers, and the award allowed me to drop half of my teaching timetable in order to carry out the research. Since teaching is only part of what lecturers do (there are vast amounts of admin, endless meetings to attend and students require plenty of support other than teaching) this meant that roughly a day and a half per week could be spent on the project.

The award was intended to be spread over two years. However, a serious chest infection in year one, followed by a frightening six months of illness in year two when a rogue virus attacked my spinal cord, added lengthy and frustrating delays. It was even more remarkable that the women participating in the research stuck with it through all these months of inactivity, and I am deeply grateful that they did. When I limped back to work with my walking stick I did find that a handful of women I wanted to interview had moved house, left college or otherwise gone out of reach. Losing touch with women who had volunteered to be interviewed saddened me greatly, and if any of you are reading this, please accept my apologies!

In the end, the whole thing was completed in just under three years.

It was intended to be a small-scale pilot project, involving perhaps twenty or thirty women, but the response to my appeal in *Diva* for interviewees (see below) was so overwhelming that it turned overnight into the largest research project of its kind. This means that the findings ought to be taken seriously by scholars around the world who are exploring sexual identity. Exciting, yes. Scary? You bet!

Stage one: picking up women everywhere

The first stage of the research lasted about six months. During this time I carried a little tape recorder everywhere I went, and interviewed women 'on the hoof' wherever I came across them. Since this period coincided with a visit to Cape Town in South Africa (to run workshops on lesbian health), I was lucky enough to collect several interviews while I was there. Since I didn't have access to a car in Cape Town, women often had to travel miles to the house where I was staying in order to be interviewed. Not only were they prepared to do this, they were thrilled to take part, and several made it clear that taking part was important to them.

Back in Britain, I collected several more tapes. It was a strange time; taking women quietly to one side at parties, conferences and dinner parties and asking if I could interview them about their sex lives! Of course, it was completely inappropriate to ask "Are you now, or have you ever been, heterosexual?" so I had to remain alert to signs of a heterosexual past in the conversation of women I met and pounce on them. Going through this process over and over again honed skills which are not often called upon in lesbian social circles!

I was always pleasantly surprised by the response I met. Nobody refused to talk with me. Women were as interested in my research as I was in their stories, and an interview would often be followed by a reversal of roles, as my interviewee interrogated me. I became intrigued by what seemed to be a mirror-image of lesbian sexuality – easy role-reversal and a concern for equal shares in the pleasure – but that is another research project altogether!

Stage two: the floodgates open

When I had 14 tapes I began analysing the transcripts, and wrote a short article for Britain's favourite lesbian magazine *Diva*. The article ended with a brief questionnaire and a plea for women to contact me if they would like to talk about their own experiences.

Now, I wasn't expecting much out of that article. I didn't think very many women would find a pen, fill in the questionnaire, cut it out of the magazine (or take it into work to photocopy), find an envelope and a stamp and post it back to me. That seemed like a huge amount of trouble to go to to help an unknown researcher and I was expecting half a dozen replies at most. I didn't even bother watching out for the article to be published.

So when I went into the university one Monday morning and found my pigeonhole stuffed to bursting point I was stunned. I locked myself away in my office and spent the entire day opening nearly forty envelopes. They didn't only contain completed questionnaires. The article had clearly hit a nerve, and women had responded with generosity and frankness. They wrote me letters, sent carefully chosen cards and even poems. Some wrote out their life story, some couples wrote a joint narrative, some told pointed anecdotes. There was an outpouring of mixed emotions: relief, anger, pain, sorrow, pride, recognition, excitement.

By the end of the day I was an emotional wreck, having been drawn into women's stories of joy, struggle and loss. Many of the letters made me cry, or gave me goosebumps. Some made me angry. The theme which ran through many of them was "Thank you for telling me that, even though I was heterosexual once upon a time, I am a 'real' lesbian now." Many women had been judged by lesbians in their local community, or had judged themselves, not to be 'proper' lesbians. Several had been too scared to venture out among other lesbians, women they perceived as the 'real thing'. I won't quote from those letters; they were intended as private communication and not for public consumption. But the experience of being judged by other lesbians and rejected as not a 'real' lesbian also came up in the interviews, and you can find out more later on in the book. Here I will just say that reading accounts of this attitude in so many letters made me see red.

The flood of communication went on for weeks. During this time I received many emails from distant lands, several bulky envelopes with foreign stamps and more life stories. Hundreds of completed questionnaires piled up in my in-tray, and dozens of women offered to take part in an interview. It was one of those magical times when it is possible to feel part of a truly worldwide community of lesbians, and I loved it. I was, and continue to be, delighted and moved that women were so eager to share their stories with me. It also made me acutely aware of my responsibilities, as a researcher and as a member of this global community, the lesbian nation.

The reponsibility to deal honestly with women and to be worthy of the generosity and trust they showed me is one which I did not take lightly. It means that I have worked very hard not to force these stories into my theories, not to edit them into meaning something I want them to mean. Weaving the strands together, trying to see a pattern and then working out the meaning of the pattern (or, indeed, whether there is a meaning at all) has been my task.

The full-length 'stories' which you will find at the end of each chapter are almost unaltered from my interview transcripts, although I have made a few small changes for clarity and ease of reading. As for the quotations which you will read scattered throughout the book, they are unchanged except where I have taken out a few words to make them less clumsy to read, as indicated by three dots. In this way I hope to give a flavour of the hesitations and complexities of real speech, while giving as honest an account as possible of what women actually said.

I have read the interview transcripts over and over again, trying to identify the key themes which emerge in them. Anything that crops up in more than half the interviews is clearly a theme of major importance. Such themes have then been worked up into chapters, each one dealing with something which a number of interviewees spoke about. Of course there were many such themes, and they could not all be fitted into this book. In deciding which themes should be included (and which should go into the more academic reports on this study), I thought carefully about who was going to be reading the book and why I was writing it in the first place.

The purpose of this book

I have written this book, as I promised the women who took part, in order to make life a little easier for women going through the transition from a heterosexual to a lesbian identity and life. For example, it seemed important to include something about how local lesbian communities can react to ex-heterosexual women who are looking for support and guidance, or about ways in which family members and straight friends can help or hinder this difficult process. So, where the question for an academic audience might be "Is this statistically significant?", the question which guided me here was "Is this information likely to make a difference to other women?"

Of course, I had to ensure that I could protect the confidentiality of everyone who took part. Each woman was given the opportunity to choose a pseudonym, and all the other names mentioned during the interviews were changed as well, to protect family members. I have also used fictional placenames, so don't bother looking 'Westchester' up in the road atlas!

At the end

As the research project drew to a close, I wanted to give something back to the women who had been so generous with their time. The budget was almost gone, but enough remained to organise three small social events around the country. Since many women had told me how isolated they felt (particularly outside London, with its vibrant lesbian scene), this seemed like a very good idea. One took place in the Glass Bar in London, hosted by the lovely Elaine, and was a great success. Women came along to meet me and each other, to chat and to show photographs of families, children and girlfriends. A second, held in my home city, attracted fewer women but was very enjoyable. I answered questions about the research and was delighted to meet women who I knew only as thoughtful voices over the telephone. The third, organised by the very wonderful Netty, took place not far from Leeds. Having managed to crush my foot in a hideous DIY accident two days earlier, I was prevented from getting there when the Virgin train I was on broke down in Sheffield, leaving me to hobble painfully back to Bristol on my crutches. Undeterred, Netty and a friend (who wishes to remain nameless) supervised what sounds like a hugely enjoyable party. I am still peeved that I missed that one!

Consequences

Over and over again, I was told that simply taking part in this research had made a difference to women who spoke with me. I also received several letters like this one:

> "Dear Tamsin,
>
> Hi! Just a note to say thank you for sending me the transcript. I have to admit it made me smile because of the way it is written (not edited)...
>
> Seriously though, I've found the whole experience quite cathartic. After you interviewed me I felt really strong, as if it was in the past and I had closed a door on a chapter of my life. It has been such a drain on me over the past four years and it feels such a relief to move on. So whereas I was initially quite scared when you first contacted me, I found it a totally positive experience, and I'm really glad I saw your article and responded to it."

It is a rare and delightful privilege to carry out research which has such a positive impact on anyone taking part in it.

Just as important is the determination shared by many of the women who allowed me to ask them such intimate and difficult questions about their lives. Time and time again, once I had turned off the tape recorder, I heard the same thing: "If doing this helps another woman going through the same thing as me, that's all I want."

This is a very generous thing to do. Even in the best of circumstances, it is not always easy to talk with a complete stranger about deeply personal matters like desire, sexual experiences, marriage breakup and traumatic life events. For some of these women – not yet 'out', living in insecure circumstances, still struggling to leave male partners or deeply troubled about the reactions of parents, employers or children – speaking to me took very real courage. I remain humbled by their willingness to trust me and their extraordinary honesty. Nobody ever said, "Oh, I'm not going to talk about that," or "That's private and none of your business." Even women who were clearly shy by nature, and finding it quite difficult to reply to some of my questions, somehow managed to come up with the words they needed. This book is my way of meeting my obligations to all these brave and generous women.

If I am honest too (and I am not about to be the only one here who's pretending), I have to say that this is not an easy thing for me to do either. For one thing, listening to these stories through three years plunged me back into the emotional turmoil of my own journey from heterosexual marriage to a lesbian identity and lesbian life. Perhaps it was good for me, but it was certainly painful, and gave me a few sleepless nights.

It is also not at all easy to defend my choice to write this book in career terms. In the increasingly insecure world of universities, academics are under a great deal of pressure to go for large research grants (seldom available for research into sexuality, let alone lesbian sexuality) and to publish their findings in specialist academic journals or textbooks. My university funded this research and they wanted something in return – theoretical articles in prestigious journals and scholarly papers presented at international conferences.

I am going to write those articles; but I am a lesbian first and an academic second. The academic papers may make a difference or they may not. In either case, any impact they may have will not be felt for a long time – probably years. On the other hand, if just one lesbian buys this book and is helped by it, I shall feel it was all worthwhile.

There were times during my own coming out journey when it all seemed unbearably hard. Times when I was trying to work out what to say to lesbians who told me I couldn't be a 'real' lesbian because I'd been married, or when my husband threatened to go to court and have our son taken away from me, or when my one-time best friend wrote to say she didn't want anything more to do with me. Plenty of times curled up on the floor sobbing, plenty of times trying to speak calmly when I was frozen with fear. During those times, a book like this one would have been a lifeline.

So I was just as determined as the women who took part in this research that their stories should be told to other lesbians first. I share their hope that this book will help other women struggling to make sense of their shifting sexuality and fighting to build a new life for themselves. I also hope that it helps make sense out of chaos for other people who are trying to support someone close to them who is going through a similar transition – be it a daughter, sister, mother, even a wife. Given that these stories refute many mainstream beliefs about what lesbians are like, perhaps it will make a difference in the wider world as well. I hope you enjoy reading these stories as much as I enjoyed hearing them.

Across continents:
Len's story

I interviewed Len in the passageway behind a noisy café in Cape Town, South Africa. Listening to the sounds on the tape takes me back there in an instant: to the heat, the cheerful bustle, the smells and sounds of South Africa's most beautiful city. It brings back the memory of suddenly realising, as I stepped off the plane from England, that I was in a country that had written lesbian and gay rights into its constitution. Ask many people about South Africa and they will tell you about the violence, the continuing poverty, a troubled and struggling land. Ask me and I will say the same things. But I will also tell you it is the country where, for the first time ever, I realised that I was safe *as a lesbian*.

Although we were a world away in geographical terms, this is a story with its roots in England. As you will see, Len's ordinary life in a small town in the North of England was transformed for ever when she met and fell in love with a woman for the first time. When we spoke, she was still with the same woman, and had moved to Cape Town in order to be with her.

Leaving heterosexual married life is difficult for any woman, and doubly hard when you are leaving as part of the process of establishing your new life as a lesbian. For Len, this involved leaving behind her children (albeit temporarily), her home town and her country of origin to follow her lover half way around the world. This makes her part of the 'gay diaspora', those lesbian and gay people who follow their hearts to places far away from their homeland. Again, this is much easier for heterosexuals, who have only to marry to ensure that their relationship is accepted by immigration officials and others. If you think partnership rights and immigration regulations are boring and unimportant issues, just keep your fingers crossed that you never meet and fall in love with someone from the other side of the world!

*

I think I prefer the word 'lesbian' to 'gay' in the sense that it's more woman-identified, as 'gay' is too broad. Personally, for me, I would prefer that word even over 'dyke'. I don't mind the word 'dyke' but I describe myself as a lesbian.

I have been in a relationship with a woman for about three years but before that (this is my first and only relationship with a woman), I would have described myself as heterosexual. I think when I first started the relationship with her I would have probably described myself as bisexual but now, going on from then, I would say clearly I am lesbian and I wouldn't consider having a sexual relationship with a man again.

It was very traumatic at the beginning, extremely traumatic. I think the best thing is if I tell you a bit about my history. I was married for twelve years and I was still married when I met my present partner, and I've got three children, but I had never questioned my sexuality; it just never came up. I did know lesbians but they weren't within my close circle of friends and I think I probably had the attitude that that's OK for them, that's their choice, but it just never came up for me. I never looked at it or explored it at all and I was very clearly... I perceived myself as heterosexual, I had several boyfriends before I got married and it was never an issue.

So when I met Jay... she came over from South Africa to England to work in the hospital that I was working at; she had come over as a doctor to do some locum work and I was staff nurse on the ward that she came to. We started off as a friendship, I was quite interested and fascinated by her. I knew she was a lesbian because she was quite out and that didn't phase me one way or the other. I was fascinated by this woman but more in the sense that she had such interesting stories to tell... It was just a complete opposite to me: that she had travelled the world, had done this and that and there was I who had been abroad a few times but only in a sense of holidays with families, never done any travelling on my own.

I had been very much the married mother with three children, from the age of about 23. I was pregnant when I got married, so I never had any married life without my children and I think it was a diversity that intrigued me and I found myself wanting to spend more time with her and listen to her and just talk to her. Not long after that, after actually meeting her, we starting spending more time together. Originally it was a group of us, but then it became more one to one.

She lived quite close to where I was living and I think she was quite lonely too, and since she was over here she knew hardly anybody. There were a couple of other South African doctors but they were male, so she didn't have any female friends. I was drawn to her and wanted to spend time with her and, during that time, I began to question why was I so interested in this woman. It seemed to me that I was beginning to question my sexuality at that stage. I was thinking that it's more than a friendship for me now, and what is this about? I was very confused, very distressed.

I think, because there was nobody who I could share these thoughts with, I was questioning myself and I was trying to get hold of literature, something to explain this process I was going through and I just remember feeling very isolated and alone and thinking I was the only woman to feel like this! As far as I was concerned lesbians knew they were lesbians from an early age, they didn't just suddenly become 35 and decide, "I am a lesbian." So then that's when I thought, well, possibly I could be bisexual. That was another option open to me and I tried to read up about bisexuality but there was nothing I could lay my hands on.

I was doing a degree in counselling at that time and I went to the medical library which was quite horrific because everything they said about lesbians and sexuality was very much medicalised, even though it wasn't on the DSM [Diagnostic and Statistical Manual][1] any more and it wasn't actually seen as a mental illness. I read that it wasn't normal and it certainly wasn't acceptable by mainstream society. I was also scared by the way that I had seen bisexual and lesbian women treated on the ward; I had seen how the nurses couldn't cope with it at all, they felt very threatened by it. I never had this problem; in fact I got quite good relationships with them. If anything I think I was more empathetic towards lesbians and bisexuals. So, probably subconsciously, I might have even been questioning then but I certainly didn't openly speak to anybody about it.

While I was going through this questioning I didn't feel as if I could share this with anybody. I was very unhappily married but not unhappily to the state that I thought I was going to leave him and have a relationship with a woman. I just knew that I didn't love my husband. I had a terrible sexual relationship with him; I was not interested in sex for the whole twelve years we were married and it was very much an issue for him that he wanted more sex than I did. He used to say that I must be a lesbian because I didn't want to have sex with him and I preferred the company of female friends to him. That's what he said; he said I was a lesbian on a couple of occasions. I firmly denied it and just said I don't want sex, it doesn't mean that I am a lesbian.

Jay must have been picking up vibes but we never spoke about it. Until one evening, when she actually put it to me; was I questioning my sexuality? I was just having a drink of beer at the time which I choked on! I can vividly recall that night, thinking to myself that I could either deny it and say, no don't be ridiculous, or I could be honest and say, yes I am, and what would be the consequences if I said that? At that time I didn't know that she was interested in me at all, I just thought she was questioning because I obviously enjoyed spending time with her.

So I said, yes, I was questioning my sexuality and things moved on very quickly from there. She said, "We have three options, you can either say, this is too much of a problem and I don't want to talk about it so perhaps it's best if we don't see each other any more, break off being friends. Or, the second option would be that we could still be friends and the third option that we could have an affair." She left that with me and said, "Come back tomorrow and tell me!"

But (this is a very condensed story!), there was lots of other trauma and stuff going off at this time. I was under a curfew; my husband said I had to be in before midnight, and it was about 11.55 when she brought this up. The next day, I didn't finish work until 9.30 and I went around to her place and she never mentioned it. It was just like this conversation we had the night before wasn't mentioned, and I was like, oh my god, what am I going to do? Because I had already decided I was going to have the affair. The idea was a three-month fling, because she was going back to South Africa. And I thought that would be the end of it; I would have had my fling and I would go back to being heterosexual! It was very clear in my head that this was what I would do. I was quite keen to do it, thinking that if I didn't do it I might regret it and I might never have the opportunity again.

Meanwhile, my relationship with my husband was over. I told him that I would remain under the same roof as him but the marriage was over and I wanted to move out of the bedroom and all that kind of stuff.

About 11.50 she said, had I made my decision, and I said, "Oh yes, I have made my decision, and I will go for the fling." And at that stage I was so anxious. On one level I wanted this fling but, on another level, I was thinking, what happens if she goes to kiss me and I want to be sick? What happens if I think I want it but actually I'm going to be quite repulsed by it? I don't know if I can cope with this. So I couldn't get out the door quick enough! Also, she was in a relationship with a woman in Cape Town, so she was going to have an affair while her partner was over there.

I went around the next day and I sat on the chair. And she said, "Don't sit there, sit here, next to me." And I thought, oh my god, this is going to be it; what am I going to do? Then the phone rang and it was the girlfriend from Cape Town. So Jay said, "Sit and read this newspaper and I want to know all about it when I come back." I couldn't tell you anything that was in the newspaper; I just sat there, very anxious. Ten minutes later she came back and then she kissed me. And I thought, this isn't repulsive at all, this is actually quite nice! But I was supposed to be going shopping, so I had a couple of kisses and off I went! A couple of days later I saw her and we went to bed then.

And it wasn't a three-month fling! At that stage I really thought it was going to be. This was in the December and when it came to February when she was going, it was still very much 'a fling'. She was going to come back to England but it wasn't going to be to my town. She was going to do an MA in Gender Studies and Women's Studies, but she had no intention of doing it anywhere near here, because the universities round here aren't that brilliant. So it was going to be London, Bristol, possibly even Scotland. When she was next in South Africa, she wrote to me a couple of times and I phoned her a couple of times. She had broken off the relationship with her girlfriend, but there were still lots of issues around where she was going to live when she came back and which university she was going to go to and also a big issue around my children.

She came back to England in April. I met her at the station and we had a weekend at a friend's and talked about what the possibilities were here. I was very unsure about what was going to happen, thinking that she wanted me but she didn't want my children, but we came as a package. During that time I was moving out of the marital home as well. I moved out the following week and she helped me with that. There was an arrangement made that I had the kids in the week and my ex-husband had them at the weekend. So we had every weekend free and she had a couple of visits at different universities and she looked round a nearby university and decided that she would go there. I think partly that was because of the location, near me, so that she could travel there and partly because she got a locum job in a neighbouring town. So from there we lived together.

By now I was thinking of myself more as a lesbian. I was leaving my options open around being bisexual, in case this was still a fling and she was going to go back. I was very much aware that I was not attracted to any other women. I was only attracted to her. This probably lasted for over a year, that I just did not look at other women in the way that she did. She would see a lesbian or a dyke walking down the street and she would say, "That's a cute dyke" or whatever, and I would say, "I really struggle with what you see here, I don't have the same feelings at all." It was probably 18 months into the relationship that I could actually look at other women and feel something for them and not just Jay.

I think I was learning to be a lesbian, and also looking at women in a different way. I never looked at women that way and I had a couple of bad reactions when I did come out to my friends. The first one, who I thought was the safest woman I could come out to, was very liberal minded. But she just knocked me for six by asking did I look at her that way, and I was just like, oh my god, is this the reaction I'm going to get from everybody? But the answer was definitely no. I didn't look at any other woman that way, only Jay.

I had a terrible experience at work within the psychiatric ward. I was ignored by the friends who I thought were friends and colleagues. Probably out of six close friends there I only had two left. At the end of it they just couldn't cope with it at all, there were big problems about that. I think I threatened them; I threatened their lives and they just couldn't understand why I would want to leave my husband in the first place, especially not to go with another woman.

Now, if I look back on my life I was very much a tomboy. I was much happier playing football with my brother and I was never very interested in playing with dolls. Stereotypes like that, that I can reflect back on. But I think I was very keen to have a boyfriend and I had a boyfriend right the way from 14 onwards. I probably had about six months in my life where I didn't have a boyfriend until I got married, and then straight from that into a relationship with Jay.

Sexually, those relationships were never very fulfilling; I never had such a good sexual relationship as I've got now, they never did anything for me. I didn't dislike it, it just was never fulfilling. It wasn't a big issue to me, I just thought I wasn't one of those women that could have orgasms. Maybe I haven't found the right way or whatever; it just never happened.

So I think sex plays a large part in why I am a lesbian. But it's also, I remember searching for this *contentment*, like I never found my contentment in the heterosexual world, but I didn't know why. I used to question, why do all those other married women friends of mine seem quite content with their lives but there's something missing in mine? But I could never put my finger on it and say what it was!

I used to go off on different tangents. I would throw myself into sport and get my contentment and satisfaction from that; maybe it was something sexual as well that I wasn't getting and I could release through sport. Then I would go off on a tangent of studying and wonder if I could better myself and get more qualifications; perhaps then I would be happier. But it never happened. But I now say that I am content with this relationship that I have with Jay!

The biological theories don't feel real to me. I certainly wouldn't say that I was born one or that it is hormonal or genetic or any of those things. When I describe my own sexuality, or how I came to be, I would say it's very much on the continuum. I believe that most people are probably born some way in the middle of the continuum, bisexual, and because of society, its pressure and the way we are actually brought up, most people are pushed into the heterosexual side. I believe that I was more open, and able to look at the more homosexual side, and to think, well, actually this is better for me, and this is my choice, that I prefer to be with a woman. So I have moved, I've moved up the continuum out of choice and that's how it feels.

It does feel absolutely positive, no regrets on that part. I've got lots of regrets, but no regrets about being with a woman. I can look at men and think, that man is an attractive, good-looking man. But that can be with a gay man or a straight man, and I certainly don't want to go to bed with him. I'm not saying that I can't look at a man and think, he's good looking, he's attractive, but I can do that with women as well now. So it has been a real shift!

Notes

1. The DSM or Diagnostic and Statistical Manual lists the diagnostic criteria for all psychiatric illnesses.

1

THIS DAWNING REVELATION: THE BEGINNINGS OF A CHANGE

"I can't pinpoint it now. It was quite gradual, but it was like this dawning revelation and I came to a point where I thought, that's it! And it was like, wow! Brilliant! But then I thought, no it isn't. I am married. I have got six kids. I am a Sunday school teacher. Why is it brilliant? It's very complicated, very confusing."
(Barbara, 49)

Life is full of *Sturm und Drang*, of stresses, upheavals and sometimes dramatic change. It has become popular to rank major life events – everything from bereavement to taking your driving test – on a scale of stress from nought to ten. The theory is that, if you add up all the points of those life events you have gone through recently, the sum total will explain why you are now a gibbering wreck in desperate need of something more than a few aromatherapy candles in your bathroom.

Fairly high up on this stress list come things like divorce, relationship breakup, moving house, changing job, having a row with a spouse or being worried about the wellbeing of your children. I have yet to come across a stress-ranking exercise that gives points for realising that you might be gay, coming out to your parents, coming out to your boss, coming out to your kids' teacher. Yet these are all daily rites of passage for most of us who don't fit snugly into the heterosexual mould.

What is more, they are all frightening and potentially dangerous things to do. You may have the most wonderful parents/boss/siblings in the world, but there can be no guarantee that finding out their daughter/employee/sister is a lesbian won't turn them into puddles of guilt or screaming monsters. The only way to find out is to do it. How traumatic is it to plan something which might result in you losing your family, your job, perhaps even your childhood home? Even for the most confident woman from the most secure and loving background, these are massively stressful events which demand extraordinary courage.

Now imagine that, on top of having to deal with all the special gay stress, you also have to deal with a selection of the traumas at the top of the ordinary, common people's stress list. This is precisely what happens to many women who come out late in life, especially if they are married and/or have children. To all the anxieties associated with coming out you may have to add getting divorced, having to move out of the family home, working out how to support yourself and your children. The legal, social and financial baggage of marriage being what it is, you may find yourself having to come out to all sorts of alarming people: your bank manager, your children's teachers, your doctor, your parents, your in-laws. You may have to do this before you have really had time to get used to the idea yourself.

Perhaps most stressful of all, you may find yourself with little control over who knows about your sexuality. Even the least malicious of husbands/ex-boyfriends can hardly be expected not to tell your mutual friends, his family and perhaps your children. A woman may find herself suddenly living a totally transformed life, one where the ground shifts beneath her from day to day and there are no familiar reference points. If you have thought of yourself as ordinary and boring up to this point, you may have precious little experience in fighting for stability in the middle of such a whirlwind.

Women who go through such cataclysmic transformations have to deal with massive amounts of stress. To make matters worse, some of the sources of support on which we lean most naturally may suddenly become unavailable. Trusted friends, the family doctor, religious advisors and parents may all be unable to respond positively to a coming-out crisis. Yet, because this remains a largely invisible experience, there are very few sources of information and precious little recognition and acknowledgement. Often, when we are reeling from the impact of a massive shift in our lives, what we most long for is to know about others who have been through something similar. What were their coping strategies? How did they feel? Did they survive? There is a self-help book for almost every life trauma you can think of, but guides to giving up heterosexuality tend to be thin on the ground.

Remember, you have just begun to think of yourself as a lesbian. You know, as yet, very little about the gay world and what it has to offer. Where do you begin to look for advice and support? In the overwhelmingly heterosexual world of ordinary suburban estates, small towns and villages, where can you get your hands on books written by lesbians? Even if you manage to find a lesbian section in the local library, the shelves are unlikely to be crammed with advice on how to leave your bloke and join a sexual minority.

This may be because ex-heterosexual lesbians find it very difficult to share their experiences. After all, most of the world regards the 'my wife left me for another woman' story with deeply prurient interest, as a staple of top-shelf pornography. There are, in any case, very good reasons to keep a low profile; perhaps to protect children from being teased or bullied at school, perhaps to avoid shocking an ill or elderly parent, perhaps a job may be at stake. Sadly, too, the lesbian community itself is often uninterested in the struggles of women leaving heterosexuality. Some lesbians may insist that such women aren't 'really' lesbians or it may be that the local scene (if there is one at all) is geared to the needs of a younger generation who are more concerned with posing, pulling and popping pills.

So what is it like? What form does the transition from heterosexuality to a lesbian life and identity take for different women? What survival strategies have women used? How have their new lesbian relationships and young lesbian identities coped with it all? The answers to some of these questions will be found in the following pages. In this chapter, let's ask, how does the process of changing your sexual identity *start*?

This seems simple, but it is probably one of the most difficult and complicated questions known to womankind! It is almost impossible to frame the question in words which don't imply a lot of assumptions from the very beginning. For example, if you ask "When did you first realise you were a lesbian?", you imply that lesbians are born, not made, and that any heterosexual experience was a mistake, an attempt to conceal the truth, or born out of a failure to recognise the 'real' lesbian self. On the other hand, "When did you become a lesbian?" seems to suggest that it is as easy to change sexuality as it is to choose a career path. "What were the first signs?" sounds as if you are checking for symptoms of degenerative illness, and it really is not ethical (although sometimes tempting) to ask "When did you realise the error of your heterosexual ways?"

I don't claim to have solved this one, and I probably found at least a dozen ways of asking. What usually worked best was asking women what word they would choose to describe their sexuality (variations on lesbian, gay woman, dyke, queer, etc.) and following this up with "And has this always applied to you?" This question was usually answered at length, and women then went on to recount the significant events which sparked off the process which had, sometimes radically, caused their lives to change direction. This, then, is what it was like.

First inklings

As might be expected, some of the women who took part described a classic scenario. They had begun to 'feel different' at a fairly young age, had found themselves attracted to girls when they should have been dreaming of boys, had repressed these frightening feelings and gone on to marry. Unhappy and unfulfilled by married life, they had finally come to terms with long-buried lesbian desires and had eventually decided to come out as themselves:

> "I was with my husband since I was 17. I wanted babies and I wanted to be normal, and he was a nice bloke. But I don't think I have ever been really sexually attracted to any man... I pushed it all to the back of my mind, thinking it was never going to happen... That's not to say that I didn't enjoy sex with my husband, because I did, but I used to think about sex with women more and more." (Charlotte, 30)

If women recognise at a fairly young age that they find women attractive, rather than men, why do they go to such lengths to repress their true feelings? There are many different reasons. Certainly, for older women, the penalties attached to calling yourself a lesbian were once far more terrifying than is generally the case today. Of course prejudice and discrimination still exist, but things have changed dramatically. For younger women it may be difficult to imagine just how bad things were, not that long ago:

> "When I was young, I thought I was a lesbian. I'm talking about puberty, around 15, 16. It was a nightmare. It was awful, terrible. It was back in the 1960s, all about homophobia. And I don't think I'm exagerating when I say it was like being a paedophile is now. It was absolutely the pits. You were made to feel it was an absolutely awful thing to do... I really felt quite disgusted. I was made to feel, by society and the people around me, that it was a disgusting thing, so I felt disgusted because I knew I was *that way*." (Margaret, 46)

Lesbianism has never been illegal in Britain, and this has led some commentators (particularly gay men) to protest that lesbians were not particularly oppressed. This ignores two important factors. The first is that it was unnecessary to pass laws against lesbianism because women were already leading such oppressed and restricted lives. Until the discovery of the contraceptive pill, and the 'sexual revolution' of the 1960s, women had almost no sexual autonomy. They were pretty much confined to the home and penalties for sex out of wedlock were severe. An unmarried woman who became pregnant might find herself shut up for the rest of her life in a mental hospital, with a diagnosis of 'moral imbecility'. We are not talking about the Dark Ages here, but events that took place in the lifetime of anyone over forty today. When policy changes in the 1980s led to the closure of long-stay mental hospitals, many of those released into care in the community were women who had been incarcerated for just this reason.

The second important point is that the law-makers who refused to make lesbianism illegal did it because they thought that the best way to prevent women having sex with each other was to stop them ever finding out that such a thing was possible. In 1921, Parliament debated a proposal to criminalise lesbianism. The records of this debate make alarming reading.[1] In the House of Commons it was thought that criminalising lesbianism would "do harm by introducing into the minds of perfectly innocent people the most revolting thoughts". This opinion was shared in the House of Lords, where lesbian love was described in the most horrified tones:

> "How many people does one suppose really are so vile, so unbalanced, so neurotic, so decadent as to do this? You may say that there are a number of them, but it would be, at most, an extremely small minority, and you are going to tell the whole world that there is such an offence, to bring it to the notice of women who have never heard of it, never thought of it, never dreamed of it."

The reasoning behind the decision *not* to criminalise lesbianism was simply that politicians were determined to prevent it happening in the first place, and believed it could be prevented most effectively by making sure women were kept in ignorance of the very possibility. The notion that secrecy and ignorance were the best defence against this 'revolting' and 'vile' practice lasted a very long time. Women who spoke to me about growing up in the 1950s and 1960s described a world where lesbianism was made to seem unspeakably terrible simply *because* nobody actually said anything. The prohibition was utterly taken for granted, both inside the family and in the wider world:

> "I knew that I loved women, but I had sufficient conditioning as I was being brought up to know that this, in my family's eyes, was wrong." (Florence, 44)

Sometimes the prohibition was active and explicit; often a parent would step in to stop a friendship between two girls becoming *too* close:

> "When I met my first 'friend', that was years ago and my mother put a stop to that. I was 16 at the time, but I knew I was different. I knew at the age of twelve." (Charis, 55)

Usually, however, there was no need for anything so direct. There was just an unspoken acceptance that you just didn't 'do that':

> "I suppose I knew since I was a teenager. I went to an all-girls school and it was not the thing to be in those days, so you got yourself a boyfriend as soon as you could." (Jill, 51)

The most frequent pressure described by many of the women, now in their 30s and 40s, was simply that of convention. As they experienced it, the assumption that all women married and had children was so completely taken for granted that it was almost literally unthinkable to question it. As Barbara put it, she didn't even think of herself as heterosexual:

> "When I was in my 20s and 30s, it's not something you think about if you're straight. You don't think, I am straight, because it's the norm. You just assume that you're not a lesbian. I suppose it's what you are *not*. I would just have automatically thought of myself as straight." (Barbara, 47)

Of course, social change came quite swiftly after the 1960s, and slightly younger women tended not to take their parents' prejudices quite so much for granted. Rather than thinking of these negative feelings as an expected norm, they can put a critical name to them:

> "Around 14, 15, 16 I started thinking about it. So it wasn't really an early thing, like quite a lot of people say they knew from an early age... but I tried to put it to the back of my mind, because I was very scared of it. My father, more than my mother, was very homophobic, racist, everything. So I tried to put it to the back of my mind. Tried to, but it reared its head every now and then!" (Michelle, 30)

This marks an important shift. Once you can put a name to such attitudes, calling them 'homophobic', you are equipped to challenge them. They can be spoken about, alongside racism and other prejudices, as something out of the ordinary, no longer the unquestionable norm. Along with these wider social shifts can come a completely different approach from one's family and friends. Several younger women described coming out to friends or family, only to find out that they already knew or suspected! Katie's parents had done their best to be helpful and supportive long before she thought of herself as a lesbian:

> "My parents said they knew before I did, and I was questioned about it from the age of 14. I always said, no, really not, thank you for asking, it's very kind you're concerned, but I am really not." (Katie, 23).

Women of Katie's generation, whose parents grew up in the 1960s and 1970s, are lucky enough to be freed from the terror that drove older women into marriage in a desperate attempt to repress their sexuality. It is easy to play down the force of this change, but the cost to this earlier generation of women was sometimes truly dreadful. Often, I found my eyes filling with tears as I listened to stories like this one:

> "Initially I thought, right, I had better buckle down here. I'd better make [my marriage] work... It was very, very difficult. It was an act, and eventually that got to me. You can only sustain that sort of thing for a minimal amount of time. First of all it hits you physically, and then it starts to break you down mentally. And desire, for me, has always been for other women. So I just found heterosexual sex with my husband invasive. Not just the penetration, etc., I found it just invasive of my personality... I tried to commit suicide. It was a very high price to pay for what is perceived as normal, what is perceived as a social norm." (Pippa, 49)

Light the blue touch paper and retire!

For whatever reason, these women had spent a greater or lesser part of their lives as heterosexual. So, what happened to set off the process of change that ended with them able to think of themselves as lesbians and live a lesbian life? Of course, each individual woman's story is as unique as herself, but they do seem to fall into a few (very loose!) categories.

For those who had been struggling to repress their attraction to women it was often simply a case of no longer being able to tolerate the strain of living a life that was so false. For others, who had never really considered themselves to be anything other than ordinary, common-or-garden heterosexuals, things were rather different. Some just fell in love, overwhelmingly and out of the blue, and were shocked that the person they were in love with was female. Some suddenly realised that the strong bond they felt with their best friend went beyond ordinary friendship. For a few, the catalyst seems to have been an emotional trauma which, for whatever reason, jolted their desires into an unfamiliar direction. Finally, a small but significant number made a conscious decision, for a variety of reasons, to become lesbians.

Women who had buried their feelings for other women, while they struggled to fit in with the conventions of heterosexuality, eventually found themselves reaching the point where it just wasn't possible to keep it up any longer. Pippa, who had tried so hard to "buckle down" and make her marriage work, was finally forced to recognise that she was dealing with things that could not be shut out by an effort of will. She explained, "I don't feel as if I have a choice, in that it doesn't work. Anything else that I have tried doesn't work." For her, as for other women in her position, coming to terms with her lesbian sexuality "is the only thing that works."

Whether or not women feel that they have any choice about their sexual orientation, there are still choices to be made about how to deal with it once it has been acknowledged. Although the emotional cost of living in a charade may be very great, it is not difficult to pinpoint the benefits of being an apparently normal, happy wife. Apart from anything else, most of the women I spoke to who had been in long-term intimate partnerships with men said that their husbands and partners were nice, decent human beings. Of course, few of them reported getting much pleasure out of the sexual side of the relationship but (with remarkably few exceptions) neither did they experience abuse or actual unhappiness. Most felt real affection for their male partners, and found it difficult to deal with the emotional fallout of leaving them. In such a complex situation much self-belief and inner strength is needed in order to move away from comfortable familiarity and into the uncertainties of life as a lesbian. Clearly, however, this bravery has real rewards:

> "I was in counselling for a while. It was hard coming to terms with it myself. Actually speaking to my counsellor and saying, 'I think I am a lesbian.' I can feel it now. I was breaking my heart. But once I said it, it was just like a ton of bricks off my shoulders. It was good, and I don't shy away from telling anyone now. I'm quite proud of who I am and what I am. It's taken thirty years to get here, and I'm quite pleased with myself, actually." (Charlotte, 30)

Florence, who had always known that she loved women but 'had sufficient conditioning' to feel she must marry, decided to take matters into her own hands when her marriage ended.

> "I thought, right, I have actually got to go and do something quite positive about this. So I decided to go and live on the South Coast. So I moved to Eastbourne, which is not quite Brighton but it's pretty good, and I went and bought a copy of [the feminist magazine] *Spare Rib*. I am now 44. I got divorced 14 years ago, so I was 30. So I went and got my copy of *Spare Rib* and basically answered an ad in the back of it, thinking, I have got to start somewhere!" (Florence, 44)

Although their lives and choices are far from easy, women who have suspected for a long time that they might be lesbians are at least not surprised by their own desires. For women who had no reason to think they might be anything other than straight, however, suddenly to find themselves in love with another women can be a total shock.

A bolt from the blue

The French, naturally, have a name for it: *coup de foudre*. When love strikes, unexpectedly, out of a clear blue sky, it can turn lives upside down as surely as a direct strike from a meteor. If you add to this familiar turmoil the shock of finding yourself, for the first time and with no prior warning, in love with a member of your own sex, things can get *really* intense.

According to all existing 'scientific' theories of sexual orientation, such things shouldn't happen. If you have a 'gay gene', gay brain structure or other biological abnormality, it is highly unlikely that this would wait until you had spent years in heterosexual contentment before manifesting itself. Yet this story turns out to be far more common than we might suppose. I found myself surprised at how often women told me something very similar; there I was, leading a normal, boring life, when, wham! I fell in love with this woman. Paula was typical in her need to stress repeatedly just how unexpected the whole thing had been:

> "I was 35 years heterosexual. It wasn't something that I ever had to think about, because I just accepted that I wasn't different. I never had those feelings of being different, I just fitted in... It was not something I ever had to think about and so when it happened to me, when I fell in love with a woman, it was just such a shock, a complete shock, and I thought, this can't be happening to me!" (Paula, 40)

Over and over again, women said similar things. Far from being something they had always secretly known or suspected, falling for a woman was something that just came along out of nowhere. Once they acted on this unexpected new desire, they discovered equally unexpected pleasures:

> "I just fell in love with a woman. It just happened! And it felt really nice and natural and close. It was a closeness that I had not felt before with anybody." (Kerry, 32)

What is also clear is that this can happen anywhere, anytime, to anyone. The significant event can be relatively mundane. Who would have thought that being off work sick would spark off a major life change?

> "It was very strange. I was off work at the time with the flu, and I just sat at the internet and started going into the chat rooms, because I was bored. I started going into the women's chat rooms for some reason, and then it started from there, really! I met this woman on the internet, and we got quite close... I ended up coming up to London to see her, and when I got back, that was when I realised and I knew I had to tell my husband." (April, 45)

In complete contrast to April's experience is the story of Louise. She recounts how her sexuality seemed to change direction as she emerged from a major depression. This was quite traumatic for her, since she is still very much in love with her husband and struggling to come to terms with the implications of her new feelings and unfamiliar self:

> "I have been married for nearly eleven years. When my son was born I had severe post-natal depression for a very long time. I was hospitalised and I was on a lot of medication for a very long time. I went off sex, basically, as one does, and the attraction with men never came back again... in some ways it was a relief when I started being attracted to people again, but I was shocked to find that they were women." (Louise, 32)

It is, of course, tempting to suggest that Louise's depression was perhaps 'caused by' deep-rooted lesbian desires that she was repressing. However, I think this interpretation says more about our own need to make untidy facts fit our reassuring theories than it does about the experience that is being recounted here. Louise herself does not believe this to be the case. In fact, she stresses how much she continues to love her husband, and how little she feels has actually changed about her inner self:

> "I don't feel personally different about it. I mean, it's something that has obviously changed. It doesn't seem to have changed me really, it's just changed who I am attracted to." (Louise, 32)

This is really something quite different from an experience such as Carol's. She found her whole life, and her sense of who she is, turned completely upside down by her first sight of a particular woman:

> "We had been married for about 15 years... Somebody moved in further down the road. And they were having one of those silly parties, and came to invite us to go.

> And I opened the door and I went boomp! For no reason at all. I had never met this person before in my life, and as soon as I saw her, I thought, trouble!" (Carol, 55)

Opening that door changed Carol's life for ever. She went on to leave her husband, came out as a lesbian and has been a lesbian ever since.

Of course, not every *coup de foudre* happens like this. For many women, it happens when the other woman concerned (who is usually already a lesbian) makes the first move. In Nicky's case, she was clearly dithering about on the lesbian threshold (having already been to Pride with the woman concerned) and it was perhaps obvious that deeds, not words, were required to get her to step over that threshold:

> "She basically grabbed me by the pyjamas and dragged me into bed, because I was sat on my bed talking, and she said later, 'I just got fed up with you waiting and not doing anything!' She grabbed me into bed and she asked, is this my first time, and I had to pretend it wasn't, and I had to be cool and say that I had slept with lots of women!" (Nicky, 38)

Sometimes, a lesbian who makes the first move seems to be responding to signals that may be unconscious or may not even be signals at all. Virginia thinks that the woman who so unexpectedly initiated her into the joys of lesbian love had been misreading what was going on: "When we were driving," she explains, "she was sitting in the back seat of the car and I was looking in my rear-view mirror at the cars behind, and she thought I was looking at her." So her no-nonsense approach to seduction took Virginia completely by surprise, although the surprise was not an unpleasant one:

> "It was completely accidental... A demonstrator was sent down to the London office to help train new demonstrators. I spent a lot of time with her, driving her around, and one day I was at the hotel where she was

> staying and we were having meetings. I had had a bit too much to drink, I didn't want to drive the car back. So I asked her if she would mind if I stayed in her room. And when I went up to her room she threw herself on me and kind of threw me on to the bed, and the next thing we were involved in this extremely passionate embrace. We spent the night together and had a very passionate night... I had had quite a few sexual relationships with men, following the end of my marriage, but I had never experienced anything like this, in terms of possibilities for a sexual, passionate relationship!" (Virginia, 44)

In this case, the 'old hand' lesbian was just as shocked as the novice, as Virginia explains:

> "She was absolutely flabbergasted and shocked to hell, because she had assumed that this was something that I had engineered, whereas for me it was something that had never crossed my mind... This woman was someone who was very beautiful... She was someone that most of the guys in the company were lusting after! I assumed she was the kind of woman who all the men were kind of having wild times with." (Virginia, 44)

Despite the fact that this intense episode of seduction was, in different ways, quite a shock for both participants, Virginia never looked back. She has thought of herself as a lesbian ever since.

More than just good friends

It is widely accepted that women can become extremely close to their best friends. During the nineteenth century, in Britain and the US, it was common to find two women so closely bound by friendship that when one of them married, the other would come along on the honeymoon! As Lillian Faderman notes, in her groundbreaking lesbian classic, *Surpassing the Love of Men,*[2] such passionate friendships were regarded as completely innocent in the pre-Freudian era. Some women went so far as to set up home, and these partnerships, called 'Boston marriages' in the US, were thought of as normal and proper. When the two ladies of Llangollen,[3] Eleanor Butler and Sarah Ponsonby, ran away to set up home together in a rural idyll in North Wales, the romance of their story became famous throughout Britain and they were visited by many of the great and the good, including the poet Wordsworth. Yet this was in the reign of Queen Victoria!

Nowadays, social attitudes towards all things sexual have moved far beyond what the Victorians could imagine, and women have attained at least enough liberation to feel confident in exploring the erotic aspects of intimacy and passionate closeness. It is, perhaps, not surprising that the affection of a close friendship should, for some women, tip over into something that they can only call falling in love. This is not an easy experience. Best friends who have led conventional lives and suddenly find they are in love with each other have a lot to lose. Apart from anything else, there is the ever-present worry, is it just me? If I tell her how I feel, will I wreck our friendship?

> "Up until then we were both straight, married, two kids, nice car, nice house, nice little village. These sorts of things don't happen, only in TV programmes. And then she said, 'I want to tell you something.' And she didn't. She kept going to tell me and didn't and didn't. And then she went on a week's holiday and we missed each other like mad. Then we told each other how we had missed each other, and we just got it together! Up until then we were normal, and having normal relationships with our husbands." (Tina, 43)

The emotional impact of falling in love is famously intense. When it happens to two women who are not quite sure what is happening, that intensity can be amplified to the point where it becomes really quite frightening, as Ann and George discovered. I interviewed them together, in the kitchen of their cosy home, and this is how they told the story:

A: We made friends through our children.

G: But we just *knew* that we had to be friends. Something deep down that said we've got to be friends.

A: From the minute we became friends, everything else was out of the window. That was before we did anything else!

G: Yes, we were friends for about two years before we ever realised ourselves, let alone confronted it. It was just the two of us, the rest of the world didn't exist, and of course the first people to pick up on that were obviously our husbands. They didn't take it seriously, not as a relationship.

A: "Another friend she has got to talk to all day long and see all evening"!

G: We both had three young children then, and husbands and mortgages and everything that goes with it. You can't deal with that. We are not the sort of people that go out and have affairs. I wouldn't do that, it's not in my makeup to deceive. And yet there was this thing that was so powerful that I had to do *something*. We lost weight, we were shaking, it was like there was something wrong with us.

A: When we look back, from the minute we said, this has changed, this is how we are, six months later we had both left home.

G: We told each other in the April, and by the September she left home. We had to do it. All the time we were living with someone we were pretending that there was nothing else going on. The worst bit was actually building up to telling the other person how you felt. Even though you knew, deep down, there was always that chance that she was going to turn round and say, no, I don't feel like that. It was me that had to say it in the end, because I was living a lie. I had to take that chance.

For anyone who has never been through that strange and terrifying process it is probably hard to understand just how deeply it can shake you. Don't forget, these are two women who have never so much as dreamed that they might be lesbians. For them, falling in love isn't about hearts and flowers; it is something that reaches in and shakes the very roots of the person you thought you were. George, her arm firmly around Ann's shoulder, spoke with great feeling about her experience of being in the grip of new and sometimes shocking emotions:

> "It's like you've found the other half. Suddenly, with all the millions of other people in the world, you've actually found that other half that, when you put them together, it's just right. But to come to terms, to accept that that other person is a woman; it was hard. Sometimes I had to block that bit out and just pretend, oh, it's a person." (George, 41)

Hearing this made me wonder how many women, living in less accepting societies, in the grip of religious intolerance or out of simple ignorance, may never be able to recognise that they have 'found the other half', just because she happens to be a woman.

Explorations and choices

At the opposite end of the spectrum were those women who, for a variety of reasons, had chosen to be lesbians. Again, science does not recognise the existence of choice in this matter. Nor, we must acknowledge, do some lesbians. If you have thought of yourself as a lesbian as far back as you can remember, and have been forced to find ways of dealing with that for most of your life, perhaps it can be galling to listen to women who insist they made a choice to be gay, of their own free will. Yet there is no doubt that, for some women, this is precisely what does happen. The reasons behind their choices, however, may be very different.

The one thing they all have in common is the simple fact that they were aware of the existence of gay people. In other words, lesbianism existed as a possibility, as something they could (at least, in theory) choose or reject for themselves. It seems that this is much easier for some of the younger generation of lesbians than it was for older women. At the ripe old age of 23, for example, Toni was able to look back on her adolescence and muse, "The first time I thought about it or considered it was when I was about 14 or 15, when I got very attached to my best friend. That was just a thought in my diary. I remember writing, maybe I'm a lesbian." Asking herself this question, even committing the thought to paper in her diary, didn't seem to cause Toni much anxiety. Things have clearly moved on since the days when Margaret was made to feel "disgusted" by the recognition of her lesbian feelings.

For Ann, the decision to choose women as sexual partners was strongly expressed as a way of looking after herself. At first she makes it sound almost as simple as any other lifestyle choice:

> "I suppose in the last two years, not as a conscious decision, I have become much healthier and I hardly drink tea or coffee and I don't smoke, I don't drink alcohol. A total change from how I was in my 20s, I abused my body in that way a lot. So I can't see the point of doing things that don't do me any good, and having sex with men came into that category." (Ann, 35)

It soon emerges, however, that her apparently simple choice is much more complex and difficult to deal with than this initial account suggests:

> "I did really fall in love with my daughter's dad. I must have done, because I was terribly hurt when he left. He's the only person that I really fell in love with, and have had that experience with. Then maybe I'm not a lesbian? After he left I was very busy being a single parent and I sort of came out as a lesbian. And yet, I think that my sexuality is bound up with reproduction and wanting children." (Ann, 35)

For Ann, the ability to be open-minded enough to think of a lesbian life as a possible option seemed to have made life very confusing and complex. After all, if there is a choice, on what grounds might you *make* that choice? Reproduction, security, emotional intimacy, sexual pleasure, your own self-esteem as a woman – all these factors and countless others might have to be considered. After discussing all these at length, Ann concluded, rather wistfully:

> "I really believe that I can choose, that I can use my sexuality for whatever purpose I want to use it. But at the same time, I think I'm very out of touch with my feelings... My sexual response is my own, I can choose. But then, you can't always, can you? You can't always choose."

One social factor which seemed to make it possible for some women to make a conscious choice to *become* lesbians was feminism. With the rise of the women's liberation movement, particularly in the 1970s, women began meeting real, live lesbians in a safe environment where they weren't pretending to be anything else. For many, the experience was entrancing:

> "I had been a struggling heterosexual. I had had lots and lots of relationships, some of them quite long, five or eight years. Lived with men. I had always been looking for Mr Right, as you do when you are heterosexual, and I actually thought I had found him. That was at the time of the women's liberation movement and I started going to an arts centre, here in London. I used to admire all these lesbians at this arts centre. And this was in the days when you had a women's disco, it got hot, and people took their tops off, so admiring a lesbian had a lot of resonance then! I just thought they were all wonderful. And then I woke up one day and thought, well, that's silly, I don't have to admire them, I can *be* one!" (Ruth, 58)

Ruth was not alone in this experience. For Louise, who was 33 when we spoke, there was something heroic about lesbians that both attracted and intimidated her:

> "I kind of aspired to being a lesbian, but I couldn't quite believe that I could actually *be* one. I could see that I was a feminist, and it was in the 1980s, when lesbians sort of appeared. Certainly my reason was that they were the heroes of the feminist movement." (Louise, 33)

For many women at that time, it was the done thing to call yourself a lesbian if, in the infamous words of the Leeds Revolutionary Feminists, you were a "woman-identified woman who does not fuck men".[4] Lesbianism had become so much about politics that you could lay claim to the political credibility of lesbian feminism without so much as laying a finger on another woman. For Louise, this was dishonest. She wasn't going to pretend that she had not felt anything for men, but nor was she prepared to call herself a lesbian unless she *was* a lesbian:

> "I knew that I had been attracted to men; those feelings were much more powerful than I had felt for girls... I didn't define myself as a lesbian before sexual involvement with a woman." (Louise, 33)

It is difficult to hear accounts such as these without concluding that an element of conscious choice was involved. Suzanne, for example, was quite clear: "When I hear people say, you're born like this and it's not a choice, well, I feel like saying, I chose this way!" For her it was not exposure to feminist ideas that led to this choice, it was simply a growing fascination with some lesbians who just happened to be part of her friendship network:

> "I think, if I'm honest, from teenage days I was totally heterosexual. And then I started making friends with a woman at the playgroup who was bisexual. I used to go round to hers for coffee and she always had lots of lesbian friends round there. It became more of a fascination really... I couldn't work out why I was feeling like this, because I was married and had two children.

> And they asked me if I would like to go to a gay club. Of course, I looked so straight, with my handbag! But I was totally fascinated by it and started secretly watching the *Out* TV programme years ago." (Suzanne, 37)

Suzanne was not the only one whose decision to become a lesbian was prompted by getting to know gay people and becoming drawn to what they saw of the gay lifestyle. Katie, who at 26 is from a younger generation, tells a very similar story:

> "Well, I had boyfriends throughout university. They were all OK but nothing particularly special, no particularly strong feelings. Then I met P, who was a long-term relationship... I went out with him for about four and a half years. I began going out with other friends, gay friends, and basically I saw that there was an alternative that people enjoyed. That they went out, and they didn't have two heads, and I thought, I'm going to try this alternative and see, and I tried it and I liked it." (Katie, 26)

However difficult it may be to try and make such experiences fit into any of our existing theories, there can be no doubt that some women are confident enough, adventurous enough and unconventional enough to 'suck it and see'. For them, being exposed to a culture that is organised around a different sexuality is, perhaps, a little like being exposed to unfamiliar foreign food. And how do you know you won't like it unless you try?

> "During my nurse training, a lot of the staff were gay and it was then that I started thinking. It wasn't a conscious thought. I just knew that I felt more comfortable with the gay women than I did with men, straight or gay... I then started going out with women. I went for a mad fling one summer after answering loads of adverts in the *Pink Paper*. I just went for it and thoroughly enjoyed myself!" (Julie, 35)

Of course if you can choose women, you can also choose men, and such choices may not be for the obvious reasons, as Helen thoughtfully concludes:

> I've always known that I was interested in women. My main sexual experiences were with men, but it was always women that I was attracted to... I did choose to relate to those with power rather than those without. I think that was what my choice was." (Helen, 36)

Helen seems to have tried very hard to manage her life so that she could have and bring up children in a stable relationship. For her, that definitely meant marriage: "The marriage," she explained, "enabled me to have financial stability to raise children." And then along came a best friend:

> "When we became friends I don't think I fancied her. That came later. I don't think that came until she was aware that she had feelings for me, and then it felt like things were pretty much mutual, and that was quite a revelation! It felt like coming home. Very natural. Meant to be." (Helen, 36)

The picture is now very complicated indeed! Clearly, some women experience their lesbian identity as a deep truth about their innermost selves, something they have no choice over. Struggling to repress this true self is like keeping raging floodwaters back behind a dam – sooner or later the dam must burst and everything gets swept away. But this could not be more different from the lives of women at the opposite extreme, those who are curious or intrigued enough to experiment in the lesbian world, decide they like it and stay. This evidence suggests very strongly that some women have very little choice in the matter and their sexuality remains an inner constant, whatever their behaviour. On the other hand, it suggests equally strongly that other women can and do choose, and that their sexuality can and does change. Louise who, at the age of 38, had been through several different stages in her life, said quite unambiguously: "I feel that I was heterosexual, and then I was bisexual, and now I am a lesbian. I feel that I definitely went through a process, that I changed."

It is certain that wider social changes have the power to influence how women live their sexual lives. Changes such as the rise of the women's movement, or the greater visibility and confidence of the lesbian and gay community, clearly made it possible for women to explore and experiment in ways that would previously not have been available to them. Theresa (35) expresses something like this when she says, "Put it this way; let's say we lived in a society which was much more primitive, I'm sure I would have just started playing around with women!" She meant that social convention had made it difficult for her to explore her sexuality in an uninhibited and open way. Social change, then, can constrain or liberate sexual expression, and can make it either possible or impossible for women to relate sexually to each other.

I don't want to dwell too much on theory here. Instead, I want to hand over to Fiona, whose story contains many different elements that have become familiar to us during this chapter.

> "It took a long time, and it's taken a lot of courage and a lot of determination. There is a fairy tale about somebody who wants to marry the fairy king, and they have to hold on to them tightly through all sorts of ordeals, and I think it is something like that. We worked together for eight years before... I just walked into the room and saw her and felt such strong feelings. Having been to a girls' school, and having had those kind of experiences, I just thought, how odd to have a crush on somebody now. And I just sat on those feelings, and soon after that I was pregnant anyway, and I suppose years went by and I felt the same way. But it took a sort of cathartic moment, really, of us being together and having to work together again, when I just realised that that was love. And if you had asked me before, is there any such thing as love, I would have said no...

"You can go on hitting yourself with the same stick, making yourself travel faster along a certain ride, and one day you stop and notice that perhaps you are going on the wrong ride and, if you take a different journey, that would be a truer one." (Fiona, 35)

On becoming a lesbian gradually: Dilly's story

There is a general perception that feminism has an important relationship with lesbianism. This is certainly so in Britain, the United States and other English-speaking ex-colonies, as well as some other European countries, where there have been strong women's movements in the recent past. There is also, of course, the sexist and misogynistic stereotype that all feminists are man-hating lesbians.

There are two sides to this offensive stereotype; the first is that women only become feminists because they are too ugly to attract a male sexual partner. The anger and fury of this frustrated rejection is what supposedly lies behind feminist anger at male power. It also enables the threat of lesbianism to be explained away by men (who might otherwise have to face up to the fact that so many women reject men as sexual partners altogether) as a pathetic and desperate strategy used only by those women who are too ugly or unfeminine to be able to get any 'real' sex and who have to fall back on a poor second best. So, there is no need for men to worry about their rejection by feminists or lesbians, because these women are so ugly that men wouldn't want them anyway.

The second strand is the claim that lesbianism is not driven by desire or by women choosing the kind of sex they find most pleasurable. Rather, it is motivated by hatred of men. This provides a handy escape route for those men who suspect that female sexuality is so overwhelming and complicated that they will never be able to master it. This fear turns lesbians into a kind of superbly skilled football team with goal-scoring capabilities far beyond those of mere males. Such anxieties would doom men to 'performing' for ever in the shadow of their lesbian opponents, people who have been unfairly gifted by nature with a better understanding of how to pleasure women than men can ever hope to achieve. Clearly this is an intolerable position for men to find themselves in. By downplaying the significance of desire and pleasure for lesbians, and by insisting that women are driven to become lesbians by a hatred of men, you kill two birds with one stone. You divert attention from your own fears of sexual inadequacy by not mentioning sex at all, and you can claim that all women, even lesbians, are motivated by their powerful feelings about men. This keeps men in the centre of things, where they belong.

It is also, incidentally, one reason why the feminist strategy of downplaying the sexual aspect of lesbianism was such a bad mistake.[5] To desexualise women in this way colluded with the myth that women are not sexually powerful beings. This myth is such an important foundation-stone of male power that the feminists who perpetuated it by insisting that lesbianism was 'not just about sex' (or, in the case of revolutionary feminists such as Sheila Jeffreys, not about sex at all[6]) were shooting themselves, feminism and lesbian liberation in the foot.

However, if you dig down past the offensive stereotypes produced by anxious men, and the more deluded sermons of anti-sex feminists, you eventually reach a bedrock position from which it becomes clear that feminism does, indeed, have crucial importance for lesbians.

Firstly, in simple socio-economic terms, it is almost impossible for women to acknowledge or act on their desires for other women without a degree of economic independence. Until very recently, most western nations were organised around the idea that, far from being people with basic human rights (let alone citizens with civil rights), women were the property of men.[7] If you are legally prevented from owning property – when even the clothes you stand up in belong to your father or husband – and when you have no possible means of earning a living, it is simply inconceivable to decide to opt out of heterosexuality. Getting married becomes, in a quite literal sense, compulsory. Around the world, particularly in some parts of the Muslim world, women continue to live within a socio-political system very much like this.[8] So some form of feminism has to have been successful for women to have the degree of simple material independence to allow them to choose with whom they have sex or start relationships.

Secondly, the so-called 'second wave' of the women's liberation movement in the 1960s and 1970s (the 'first wave' being the original struggle for the vote and other rights by the suffrage movement) created a counter-culture with its own infrastructure – newsletters, women's groups, magazines (such as *Spare Rib* and *Ms*), independent bookshops and publishing houses and social events such as women-only discos – which enabled women to consider the possibilities of entering into sexual and emotional relationships with other women.

The importance of this cannot be overestimated. For all its failings as a safe haven for lesbians (and they were many), the women's movement simply made it possible for thousands of women to explore lesbian life. In addition, many lesbians put a lot of energy into political and activist work within feminism. So, straight women who joined women's groups, who campaigned on a vast range of feminist issues or who simply preferred to socialise with other women (something quite unheard of until then) came into contact with real, live lesbians for the first time.

When lesbians were forced to remain a largely secret, hidden body of women it was easy to maintain the myth that they were very rare animals indeed. Once the women's movement had created a counter-cultural space where it was safe for lesbians to come out, it became obvious that there were lesbians everywhere that there were women. Though, of course, some people continue to have great difficulty accepting this basic truth!

Since feminism and lesbians have been so important to each other, the issue of feminism was one I wanted to explore with the women I interviewed. How important had feminism been to them, personally? What contact, if any, had they had with the women's movement, and what influence had this had on their ability to choose a lesbian life? It will come as no surprise to anyone that it was generally the older women who pinpointed the importance of feminism in their lives. Younger women, with a few exceptions, took their independence so much for granted that they tended not to mention feminism unless prompted.

Dilly, who was 42 when I interviewed her, gives a particularly thoughtful account of the way in which being a lesbian and being a feminist intertwine in her life. Far from being the rabid man-hater of male fantasy, hers is a story where feminist activism and growing intimacy with women develop with great subtlety, and she continues to speak of men with gentleness and affection. It is a remarkable story.

*

I call myself a lesbian. I might use 'dyke' among my other lesbian friends, but I think 'dyke' is a special word. I wouldn't expect a heterosexual person to call me a dyke. But I quite like the word amongst friends, so 'dyke', 'lesbian' are OK. I have, over the years, come to dislike being called a gay woman, because to me 'gay woman' sort of describes non-feminist lesbians really, what I call straight lesbians. Meaning women who don't have any politics around their sexuality. Which is fine, but I am not one of them. So 'gay woman' seems not quite to fit.

I started a relationship with a woman in 1984, when I was about 28, and what I started saying to myself initially, and to other people, was that I had just increased my potential for sexual partners by 100%. I didn't know at that stage, if that relationship ended, if I would next be in a relationship with a woman or a man. But by the time it ended it was fairly clear to me that I preferred to be orientated towards women. So by the end of that year I had claimed that description for myself. Even though I did subsequently have a 'quickie' with a man a few years later, that didn't significantly change the way I felt about myself.

I don't like the label 'bisexual'. I think it's a cop-out. What I find interesting is that I don't think I have ever met a woman in a relationship with a woman who insists on calling herself bisexual. I think that women in relationships with men like to call themselves bisexual if they've ever had a thing with a woman, and I think it's very suspect really! I don't like it. I think we all have the potential; we are all polymorphously perverse in my view, and therefore we may as well identify ourselves in terms of what we are doing at the time. I suppose if somebody was actually concurrently in a relationship with a woman and a man I might feel more sympathetic to that label!

If you were to ask me how I feel about myself, then I would say that I certainly could envisage having sexual feelings towards men if I was in an environment where there weren't any women. I'm not completely, as many of my lesbian friends are, repelled by men or by penises particularly; I just prefer women.

Before 1984 I thought of myself as heterosexual. But I also, for a long time, had never been afraid or had any bad feelings about lesbians. I was looking at an old diary recently, from when I was about twenty, and I had actually written something like "Have decided I am going to have a really good look at women and see whether I could imagine feeling sexual about them." I was obviously very curious! I obviously thought it seemed like a good idea, because my relationships with women have always been very passionate and close and my relationships with men have, by and large, never been that good. I have never really had... Well, I have had a few close male friends but they are not worth mentioning compared to a number of close women friends that I have.

So, I identified with 'heterosexual', even when I began to have lesbian friends. I had one close lesbian friend a long time before I came out as a lesbian, and she is still my friend now. She is a 'virgin lesbian', never had sex with a man, and she used to tease me and say, "I can't understand why you're not a lesbian." She was very pleased and relieved when I came out, she always thought that was what I ought to do.

A lot of people used to assume I was a lesbian anyway, I think, just because I was a feminist and I didn't wear makeup and behaved in a slightly more assertive way. Just like most young women who were feminists began to do in the 1970s, not behaving in the expected way.

I was a very miserable teenager. I think that one of the ways that I established my profounder footholds for myself was by being a little bit eccentric. Because I felt that I was unattractive I took to wearing quite eccentric outfits, and that was a way of establishing a different sort of identity. I think I always felt drawn to being a bit different, and to be interested in difference and not afraid of it. So I think the idea of having a different sexuality was always appealing. Not particularly that I felt I would be drawn to it for myself, I was quite happy to be heterosexual, but just generally the idea that people could be very diverse appealed to me. Once I became politically active as a feminist, which was when I was about 18 or 19, I just increasingly became oriented towards women, to do more and more things in women's company and in women-only company. So I became more and more exposed to lesbians, and women who were comfortable around lesbians and all that kind of thing. Feminism was key, yes, absolutely!

I don't know about the first time I ever became aware there was such a thing as a lesbian, but I do remember Dusty Springfield in her first manifestation, before she disappeared. I must have been not more than ten or eleven or maybe younger than that. A girl, one of my acquaintances at home, made this allusion to her and told a joke: "Mummy, Mummy, what's a lesbian? I don't know dear, I'll ask Daddy when she comes home." and I remember asking the other girls what a lesbian was, and they said it was a woman who goes out with other women. Which seemed to be an interesting and curious idea, and I imagined a very butch/femme kind of set-up.

That's what I very first remember. Then I remember there was a film on at the local cinema, a film of Mary McCarthy's book *The Group*. I said to my mother that I wanted to go and see it. She had a friend there, and they obviously assumed that I didn't know the word 'lesbian', and my mother said to this friend, "I think that's about lesbians, isn't it?" She didn't say anything awful, like, how disgusting, she just said, "Oh yes, I think it is." That's when I first remember the concept entering my consciousness.

But I don't know if there was a moment when I made a decision to be a lesbian. I think, usually when I make decisions it is something that is an organic process. I will realise that I have already made it, rather than saying, I'll do this or I'll do that. It's more of a recognition of a process that's reached completion. It just seemed obvious, really, and infinitely preferable by that time.

Actually, before I became a lesbian I was already moving in circles where loads and loads of the women were lesbians, and there were lots of really great things happening, like women-only discos constantly, and women's nights at the local pub. Things that I was very involved in. And I was also involved in all sorts of campaigns and god knows what. So it was just obvious! It was like, well, if I was going out with a man, what would I do with him? He wouldn't be able to join me in most of my social life; he wouldn't fit!

That had already started happening when I was in a relationship with a man. He felt as though he was at the bottom of my list of priorities and he felt squeezed out. Although he had very good politics, he understandably got a bit hurt by being excluded from mine. Poor man!

So it wasn't that suddenly I thought, yuk, I couldn't face a penis or even, yuk, I don't like men any more. It was more like, well, what's the point really? Why have relationships with men when I know that I can feel so much more comfortable and easy with women? I think my sexual feelings are certainly strongly and passionately oriented towards women, but there's never been a point when I thought they couldn't possibly be oriented to men again. I mean, now it seems a most peculiar idea to be sexual with a man, but that's been a gradual process which is now as much to do with unfamiliarity as anything else, I think.

So no, it wasn't for me that I suddenly thought, god, sex with women is absolutely fantastic and sex with men is crap. It was something more *whole*, really; sexual feelings being a part of it, being so much more comfortable. I felt so much more comfortable about being sexual in a social sense when with women, I no longer felt frightening or predatory or embarrassed.

I do think the greater media visibility of lesbians has made absolutely no difference in terms of the homophobia that we all experience on a day-to-day basis. I hear heterosexual people saying, yes, well, now it's acceptable. In fact, heterosexual people who really should know better! In my therapy training there were two of us, a gay man and myself, in a group of about twelve. Even in that group, you know, therapists, people who should know better, were saying, "Goodness me, I didn't realise that you still experience prejudice." And I'm thinking, what world do they live in? Well, they live in a world where *Gaytime TV* is on now, or there are a few gay films around, and they think that has made a difference!

I think, probably, on an individual basis, in terms of role models and there being an awareness in the wider community that there are lesbians about, it is easier for a young person wanting to come out now. So yes, in a personal way, but I don't think it has made any difference on a larger scale. I don't experience any less difficulty walking down the street with my partner than I would have done ten years ago.

My role models would probably have been famous feminists, women I revered, like Adrienne Rich, Audre Lorde and Bea Campbell, and women whom I had recognised within my own community as lesbians whom I thought were rather wonderful. I can't think of anyone famous in the world of showbusiness or anything, because I am too old to have had people like Jodie Foster as a role model, gorgeous baby dykes like that. There probably were lesbians around at the time, but we didn't know about them.

Notes

1. For full comment on this debate, see Esther Saraga, 'Abnormal, Unnatural and Immoral? The social construction of sexualities', in Esther Saraga (ed), *Embodying the Social: Constructions of difference*, Routledge, London, 1998.
2. Lillian Faderman, *Surpassing the Love of Men: Romantic friendship and love between women from the Renaissance to the present*, The Women's Press, London, 1985.
3. See Elizabeth Mavor, *The Ladies of Llangollen: A study in romantic friendship*, Penguin, Harmondsworth, 1971.
4. This controversial pamphlet from the Leeds Revolutionary Feminists is reprinted in *Love Your Enemy? The debate between heterosexual feminism and political lesbianism*, edited and published by Onlywomen Press, London, 1981.
5. For an overview of this heated debate, see Tamsin Wilton, *Finger-Licking Good: The ins and outs of lesbian sex*, Cassell, London, 1996.
6. See Sheila Jeffreys, *The Lesbian Heresy*, Spinifex Press, Melbourne, 1993.
7. See Harriett Gilbert and Christine Roche, *A Woman's History of Sex*, Pandora, London, 1987.
8. For information about lesbian rights in Muslim countries see Rachel Rosenbloom (ed), *Unspoken Rules: Sexual orientation and women's human rights*, Cassell, London, 1996.

2

A DIFFERENT PLANET: FIRST SEX WITH A WOMAN

> *"When I am attracted to a woman... The only way I can describe it is it's like being high on drugs, so you get this buzz. It's completely on a different planet, it's just a real high. And again, it's more than physical, definitely more than physical, and I can only think it's a cross between physical, emotional and mental. So, when I am physical with a woman, everything is heightened by loads, whereas with a man it was just physical." (Paula, 40)*

By definition the most significant difference between lesbians and non-lesbian women is that lesbians prefer to have sex with women rather than men. Indeed, this preference is so strong that women are prepared to risk a great deal in order to fulfil their desires. In many parts of the world, women continue to be imprisoned, deprived of their children, beaten or killed for the crime of having sexual contact with each other. While such punishments are not part of statute law in Britain, family courts did regard lesbians as unfit mothers until very recently and routinely handed their children over to fathers, grandparents or other family members to 'protect' them from their mothers' sexuality.[1]

Even though the legal system is gradually becoming less punitive towards lesbians, social attitudes have not always followed suit. Many people remain deeply uncomfortable about homosexuality and may feel quite justified in openly expressing their disgust and hostility. As we know from recent studies,[2] lesbians still get attacked and spat at in the street, still experience discrimination at work[3] and may still face real problems in their dealing with schools, whether as pupils or as parents.[4] If you are lucky enough to live in London or Manchester you may experience tolerance and acceptance for much of the time. If you live in the right part of town and work in the right kind of job, you may be able to forget that homophobia exists. But most lesbians do not live in the right parts of London or Manchester, and life can be much tougher in less liberal cities. It can be very tough indeed in small towns, 'respectable' suburbs and rural areas.[5] The price you have to pay for choosing another woman as your sexual partner may be high.

Given that this can be so, why do we bother? Wouldn't it be much easier to give in and fit in, to get the widow's pension and the life insurance, to go off to parents' evenings or the toddler group without worrying about what may happen to our kids if word gets out that their mum is queer? If you pile all the difficulties of a lesbian life on one side of the scales, what can you put on the other side that tips the balance and makes it possible to put up with the difficult stuff? Can sexual preference really be *that* strong? We are about to find out.

Women and sex: a very strange history

When you try to ask questions about women and sex, you quickly run into problems. This is especially so if you are interested in exploring women's desire and pleasure, since these two things weren't discovered by science until, oooh, around last week sometime. Well, perhaps it was *slightly* longer ago than last week, but not much. Until very recently, academic expertise was pretty much a men-only achievement. As feminist scholars such as Dale Spender have pointed out,[6] this meant that anyone speaking with authority about almost any subject under the sun was a man. This has been particularly troublesome when the object under scholarly scrutiny was anything to do with women, and perhaps most of all, when discussion turned to women's sexuality.

Male 'experts', including doctors and psychiatrists, long insisted that human females do not normally experience sexual desire or enjoyment. They claimed that women have no interest in sexual pleasure and only put up with sex in order to get children. This 'doctrine of female sexual anaesthesia' was taught to doctors in medical schools. They learned that women lacked the physiological and emotional capacity for sexual pleasure, were incapable of experiencing desire, and were at the mercy of a biological drive to reproduce. These archaic beliefs survived well into the first half of the twentieth century and caused much misery and heartbreak.[7] Untold numbers of women and their husbands (it was, of course, always husbands) were taught that any sign of sexual enjoyment in women was unnatural, and should be taken as evidence of moral or physical degeneration.

The medical profession saw it as its proper business to keep ordinary people in ignorance of all things sexual. In the days before mass media, this was fairly easy to ensure. So successful were they that early twentieth-century America and Britain saw the extraordinary phenomenon of the 'virgin wives', married women who consulted their doctors anxiously wondering why their ill-informed attempts at intercourse had not managed to produce babies.[8] To later generations, swamped on all sides by explicit advice about sexual technique, it is hard to imagine the misery and humiliation of those who believed semen should be deposited in the navel or the urinary tract (ouch!) and who were completely ignorant of the existence of the vagina, let alone anything as sophisticated as a clitoris.

In this climate, the trail-blazing researchers who dared to interview women about their sexual experiences quickly became household names; starting with Alfred Kinsey whose *Sexual Behaviour in the Human Female* was published in 1953.

Suddenly, the female orgasm was being talked about everywhere. The sexual revolution of the 1960s took off, the clitoris was 'discovered', and every underground magazine carried adverts for vibrators. Germaine Greer wrote *The Female Eunuch*[9] (published in

1970) in praise of female sexual power (although she didn't much like the idea of lesbian sexual power), and sexuality became a key theme for the women's liberation movement. A new generation of sex researchers, including Shere Hite and Nancy Friday, went on to explore women's sexual experiences from a feminist standpoint.

This research exposed an uncomfortable secret which lay at the heart of heterosexuality and which, with hindsight, made it clear that the sexual revolution had been much more fun for men than it had been for many of their female partners. Of course women *could* experience sexual pleasure and desire, but for most women, most of the time, sex was not particularly exciting. This depressing finding seems not to have changed much, despite the explosion of interest in sexual technique. Books, videos, films, television programmes and the internet all offer the most explicit and detailed advice on erotic fulfillment, yet it has become a cliché that sex is a great disappointment for most women.

Many of the women interviewed by Shere Hite reported that even the supposedly momentous event of losing your virginity was tedious or unpleasant.[10] Every authority who has written about this subject since the reinvention of the female orgasm in the 1960s seems to agree; first time round, don't expect it to be fun, girls. One young woman interviewed by British feminist researcher Angela Hamblin gives a fairly typical account: "I was seventeen. My boyfriend persuaded me to go upstairs at a party. It was all over very quickly and I got no satisfaction. I wasn't even that willing."[11]

Similar joyless stories can be found in any bundle of interview transcripts or completed questionnaires collected by the growing number of researchers who have explored the intricacies of female sexuality. The implication of this sizeable mountain of expert verbiage is that women's sexual responses are so strange, our sexual anatomy so complicated and mysterious, that it takes years of practice and a degree in clitoral studies to make a woman come. Female sexual pleasure is no longer regarded as non-existent or unnatural but it seems it continues to elude many women.

If sexual pleasure is problematic for women generally, the whole idea of lesbian sexual pleasure is still more complicated. Many heterosexuals – women as well as men – cannot quite work out what lesbians *do*. For one thing, they find it hard to imagine how anyone could have sex without a penis around. "One vagina plus another vagina equals zero" as David Reuben smugly put it in *Everything You Always Wanted to Know About Sex* (Bantam, 1969). In addition to this little puzzler, women are traditionally supposed to be the passive or responsive ones in sex. Men do the chasing, take the initiative, and women respond (or not). This myth is clearly so powerful that even lesbian psychologist Margaret Nichols believes it to be true; "Two women together," she writes, "each primed to respond sexually only to a request from another, may rarely even experience desire, much less engage in sexual activity."[12]

You may think this is a miserable enough picture of lesbian sexuality, but worse was to come. Faced with this disempowering account of lesbians as too feminine to start anything and lacking the necessary equipment in any case, lesbian feminists fought back throughout the 1970s and early 1980s – by insisting that lesbians had nothing to do with sex at all. There were two strands to this argument. The first can be seen most clearly in Lillian Faderman's ground-breaking and much-loved historical study *Surpassing the Love of Men,*[13] in which she argues that passionate 'romantic friendships' between women in the past were almost certainly not sexual. It was probably not her intention to desexualise lesbianism, but this was how her book was interpreted by many.

The second, and far more deliberate attempt to divorce sex from lesbianism came from a vocal strand of revolutionary lesbian feminism, typified in Britain by Sheila Jeffreys[14] and by a small group calling itself the Leeds Revolutionary Feminists. From this perspective, a lesbian was defined as "a woman-identified woman who does not fuck men".[15] Sexual desire, sexual activity or the sharing of sexual pleasure between women was, according to a statement produced by the Leeds group, "not compulsory".[16] The emphasis here was not on the erotic empowerment of women. Rather, it was on constructing a 'feminist' sexuality entirely purged of anything reminiscent of men. Since tradition had gifted men with all the best bits of sexuality this left feminists precious little to play with. Indeed almost everything that women were doing in order to explore and empower lesbian sexuality – producing lesbian porn, experimenting with lesbian-made sex toys, writing and speaking about lesbian sex – was from this perspective *not* lesbian, because not feminist enough.

This peculiar history places quite a burden on lesbian sex. First of all we can't enjoy sex because we are women, and women just don't. Then, we can't even *have* sex, because how can you have sex without a penis? What's more, even if we did want it, we couldn't do anything about it, because we have to wait for 'him' to make the first move, and there isn't a 'him' around to help us out. Finally, if we are *real* lesbians, we don't want anything to do with sex anyway, because it is all far too male-identified and unfeminist. Clearly, then, it is quite impossible for lesbians to enjoy sex. And, if it's sex and you're enjoying it, it can't be lesbian sex. Got that?

All this... and it's the first time

Given this miserable state of affairs it should then be remembered that having sex for 'The First Time' is particularly likely to be joyless and unpleasant. Indeed, if the first taste of 'normal', socially sanctioned sexual activity is so unappealing for so many heterosexual women, how much more alarming it must surely be for those brave souls who pluck up their courage to try lesbian sex for the first time. Or, as a heterosexual male colleague asked me recently, "Isn't it absolutely terrifying?" Relying purely on personal experience, I had to disappoint him. No, to be perfectly frank, terror was the last thing on my mind. Of course, there were anxious moments – what if I didn't like it after all? What if some bogeyman of childhood guilt jumped up and ruined it all? But the first time with any new partner is always a little anxious. In the end, losing my lesbian virginity was simple, pure delight. And as for not enjoying it, my chief worry was that I might be found dead the next morning from too much pleasure. What a way to go. But what would they put on the death certificate?

But I might well be a freak amongst women. I had, after all, somehow managed to enjoy dispatching my heterosexual virginity too. This in itself makes me a statistical deviant and untrustworthy as a representative of my sex. So finding out how other lesbians managed this crucial rite of passage was a key element in my research. How do women experience their first sexual encounter with another woman? Is it generally disappointing, as one might expect from the standard heterosexual story? Is it a pleasureless, orgasm-free event that makes women realise how much they have to learn before they finally achieve Sapphic bliss? Do they, trapped in their programmed passivity, lie there in growing frustration waiting for someone to make the first move? Actually, no.

What was it like the first time?

Of all the women I spoke to, two of them had not yet acted on their desires and could not, therefore, provide any information on this point. One or two others simply didn't want to talk about sex, either because other elements seemed more important or because of difficult circumstances in their current lives. And one woman recalled, with amused horror, that her first lesbian sexual encounter was "horrible", because both women were novices and "neither of us knew what to do!" But, with the exception of this handful, first-time lesbian encounters were described as being very pleasurable. Given the circumstances, this is really rather extraordinary.

The accounts are remarkably consistent. To a greater or lesser degree all of them describe this supposedly terrifying rite of passage in the most contented and glowing terms. It may not be fun first time round with a man but it most certainly seems to be when two women are involved.

> "... It was like coming home. It just felt so right. It was the first time for sexual desire and sexual satisfaction and feeling that I was doing what I wanted to do, in the right place with the right person. [I could] fall into it, plunge into it, thoroughly immerse myself and enjoy it." (Robbie, 48)

> "I'd never felt desire before. I'd never felt any of that before. It was mind-blowing that you could touch somebody and make them practically faint with wanting them. I had never felt that in my whole life. I couldn't believe it... After I realised that, I just felt like an alive person. That's how I felt; suddenly I was me!" (Catherine, 40)

It is important to remember that, for all these women, this was indeed a significant moment in their lives. They were, after all, trying something completely new and unfamiliar. There was always the risk that it wouldn't feel right for them, that they might not like it. For Michelle, going to bed with a woman for the first time was, indeed, "very scary. I thought, what if I was wrong? What am I going to do about it?" Given the amount of anxiety this would generate, the evident pleasure they experienced is quite extraordinary. Florence expressed this very clearly:

> "... It was a question of, well, let's go and see if this is right, and this is me, and this is where I need to be... I went to bed with her and I realised that this is what sex can be like, and it can be good and, yes! It's fun and comfortable and all the things it had never been before." (Florence, 44)

That final phrase of hers, "all the things it had never been before", expresses a feeling that is repeated over and over again in the interviews; *at last* women could understand all the fuss about sexual pleasure. There is a strong sense running through these accounts that sex has been a big disappointment. It has failed to live up to the hype; it has not been the overpowering, transcendent experience they were led to expect. Until now, that is.

The earth moves – at last

Often, trying to describe what had clearly been an overwhelmingly powerful discovery, women struggled to find the words. Their voices on the tape often fall silent for long periods of time, as they trawl through the language to find some way of expressing this marvellous, joyful new discovery.

> "The desire is there. What can I say! But the earth moved, suddenly all those clichés made an awful lot of sense to me. It was brilliant. It was everything I wanted and more. I never wanted anything else. It was earth-shattering." (Hilary, 37)

It was particularly moving to witness the joy of some of the older women who had discovered, at last, possibilities for pleasure that had been locked away in their bodies for many years.

> "I had a sexual awakening at 44, without doubt, and I am still learning. My body is still learning. I think it's going through a sexual maturation that it should have gone through when I was maybe 17, 18. It's just waking up. It's learning to respond and it gets better all the time. It is learning all the time and it's great! Incredible!" (Sue, 44)

Of course, the discovery of such glorious new sensations may be extremely poignant when they come along later in life. May mused, sadly, "I regret lost years. I wish I had known a long time ago. I am getting old and past it now, and I've not started yet!" Making love with a woman for the first time, at the ripe old age of 39, had been a revelation to May. Sex with men had left her so unmoved that she had concluded she must be frigid or prudish, or that there was something wrong with her.

For these women, the kind of sexual pleasure they discovered in their encounters with a woman partner was dramatically different from the pleasure they had experienced with male partners. Florence, a 44-year-old nurse, had never had an orgasm despite having been married. "It wasn't until I went to bed with a woman," she told me, "that I knew what an orgasm was." This was certainly not the case for everyone. Many had experienced satisfactory sex with male partners. Nevertheless, sex with a woman partner was described as more pleasurable in terms of aesthetics and sensation, more satisfying in terms of techniques for arousal and producing orgasm, and more exciting in terms of desire:

> "Well, sex is the best I have ever had. It's wonderful, it's very natural, very good, very exciting, very passionate. And I never got any of that from a man. Not even my husband, who I still love to pieces, but bedroom activities with him were... well, I could almost be doing a Waitrose shopping list at the same time." (Liz, 39)

So what is it about lesbian sex that is so exciting it can drive all thoughts of grocery shopping from a woman's mind? Experts such as Calderone and Johnson, who write sex manuals, reassure their readers that "the ways in which homosexual men and women express their sexuality are essentially those by which millions of heterosexual couples also express theirs".[17] In other words, sex is sex is sex, whatever the gender of those involved. If this is the case, then why should the sex or gender of a sexual partner be of any significance at all?

Experts who have tried to answer this question theoretically have tended to produce rather unsatisfactory explanations. Thus, for example, one theory about the pleasures of lesbian sexuality suggests that being weaned from the breast rather too young leads certain individuals to seek to replicate the lost pleasures of suckling at the nipple by sucking at the nearest available clitoris instead. Why any such traumatised individual, finding herself in bed with a woman, would go for clitoris-as-nipple-substitute rather than – er – nipple, is not discussed.

Luckily, we don't have to fall back on scraping the barrel of Freudian theory, since the women who spoke to me were very frank about their experiences of sex with male and female partners. Oddly, none of them mentioned weaning trauma (though I must admit that I didn't ask).

When I analysed their interview transcripts, with the intention of isolating those characteristics which distinguish men from women as sexual partners, three thematic clusters, discussed below, emerged very strongly. They are: the enhanced ability of women's bodies for sexual pleasure (multiple orgasms, more diffuse sensuality); women's greater potential for emotional intimacy; and a specific erotic 'feedback loop' produced by the experience of making love to someone whose arousal is very similar to your own (being able to imagine her arousal echoed in your own body amplifies both desire and sensation).

Women's bodies are 'nicer'

There seem to be three reasons why women find women's bodies more enjoyable than men's, although not all of them are present in all accounts, nor are they present equally strongly. The first is aesthetic. It is to do with enjoying the visual spectacle of a female body and with the absence of certain sensory features of male bodies (specifically semen and the smell of stale sweat).

> "I felt really comfortable. I always experienced sex with men as being a particular aim to a particular end that was to do with them, and quite often it was a 'lie back and think of England' job while they got on with it, really. Whereas I felt, with a woman, that it was much more comfortable. There was more time, it took longer, it felt nicer, it felt more natural. There were no smells particularly... I have never liked the smell of semen; I found that a turn-off completely, and it just felt really nice and comfortable and round. I think that was the other thing, that women are round and there were no angles! But also, it took a lot longer and it was much more satisfying than it had been before." (Elizabeth, 45)

The second element is about the erotic capacity of women's bodies; in particular the ability to engage in sexual activity for extended periods of time, the capacity for multiple orgasms, and a sexual sensitivity experienced as more generously distributed over the body than men's. In contrast, men's sexual capacity was experienced as narrowly focused on the penis and penetration, orgasm-oriented and time-limited:

> "Detached is a good word [for men]. To them, you go to bed, right then, we will have sex tonight. And that's it. Once they've done that, for them that's it. But, I mean, when we go to bed it lasts forever! You can't actually say, what time did we have sex, because it's not like that." (Georgie, 41)

The third element linked to enjoyment of women's bodies is to do with a strong sense that it is more possible to trust the technical skills of a woman, who has – in a strangely literal sense – 'insider knowledge' of the sexual workings of a female body:

> "It's almost an intuition... It's about bodies, it's about minds, it's everything. Our bodies are the same, we know where to touch. It's like reading a familiar map." (Pippa, 49)

So this is the first part of the answer. It is quite simple. Women have nicer bodies. Female bodies, with their aethetically pleasing lines, less offensive odour, whole-body sexual responsiveness and capacity for repeated orgasm, are experienced as more pleasure-giving than male bodies.

Intimacy: not like an alien, animal experience

Even more strongly significant than these physical pleasures was the emphasis on intimacy. Indeed, this enhanced enjoyment of sex is closely related to the greater capacity of women for intimacy. This seems to produce a greater sense of safety and of emotional closeness and this, in turn, is regarded as a prerequisite for sexual closeness. Given that, for women, sexual activity is associated with dangers on every front – physical, emotional, social, cultural – it can hardly surprise us that feelings of safety and emotional closeness act so strongly to enhance and reinforce sexual pleasure.

> "It was the intimacy you can have with a woman; there is no comparison. You have got that intimacy with women. I think men are from a different planet! They are! As far as sex is concerned they definitely are. It's not close. Physically they might be, but mentally they're not in tune at all. Whether they are with each other or not, I don't know." (Georgie, 41)

For many women, it is impossible to separate out their feelings about men's physical appearance from the lack of intimacy and closeness they experienced in sexual relationships with men. There is almost a sense of relief in the way they talk about lesbian sex, and about being able to experience such strong intimacy as part of a sexual relationship.

> "The wonderful bit I always read about and I had expected when I had sex with my husband was that we would be entwined as an emotional thing and on a zingy level when we were actually together and having sex. It never happened." (Zara, 39)

Nor is this inability to 'do' intimacy getting any better with the younger generation of men. Lesbians in their 20s were just as likely as older women to describe men as emotionally inadequate:

> "Basically I enjoy women's company a whole lot more and, in terms of attraction and sex, I enjoy the intimacy that you share with a woman. I just feel that they are more *there*. It's not like an alien, animal experience." (Kate, 26)

The importance that women attach to intimacy in romantic relationships is, of course, well known. It is also no secret that, in the industrialised societies of the West at least, it is commonplace for men to have great difficulty understanding what women mean by 'intimacy' and even greater difficulty achieving it. What these women seem to be saying so clearly is that the experience of intimacy is profoundly erotic and, on the other hand, sex *without* intimacy is something they find hard to enjoy. In Kate's words, it can be "an alien, animal experience". It is not suprising that women, whose socialisation (unlike that of men) actively encourages the skills associated with intimacy, are able to offer each other closer, more emotionally intense sexual contact.

Knowing me, knowing you: aha![18]

The final strand running through these interviews is about the unique experience that comes from sharing similar bodies. These accounts are particularly intriguing, given that it has become very much received wisdom that desire requires *difference* if it is to exist at all. This belief is expressed in common phrases such as 'opposites attract' or '*vive la différence*'. This is why baffled heterosexuals, unable to see where '*la différence*' might lie between two people of the same sex, assume that one must be 'the man' and the other must be 'the woman'. However, what crops up in the experiences reported in these transcripts is that *sameness*, rather than difference, can be very exciting.

For these women, sameness is something deeply appreciated, valued for the sense of familiarity and comfort and *as well* enjoyed for the spiralling intensification of pleasure which it introduces into sexual encounters between women. The complexities of the female body, which act as a barrier to understanding and intimacy between opposite-sex partners, clearly enhance sexual and intimate relationships between women. They do this in two ways. Firstly, by removing the need for constant explanation. Women need to explain to men where a clitoris is and what to do with it, what it is like to go through the physical and emotional shifts of menstruation and menopause. They don't need to do this to the same extent with other women:

> "I think it is, probably, that a woman can sense more of what another feels than a man can sense what a woman feels. For instance, PMT; a man will say, oh, he understands how you feel. A man can never understand how you feel, because he would never have it. Whereas with another woman, you could say, god I've got terrible PMT today, and she would know exactly what I meant." (Jane, 53)

Secondly, engaging in sexual activity with someone whose body and sensory responses mirror one's own can lead to an erotic feedback-loop effect which may heighten both physical sensation and the sense of emotional closeness. This can be extraordinarily intense, and trying to describe what it is like left some women literally speechless:

> "Well, I mean! The sense of these wonderful breasts that you could put your (breathless pause). This wonderful body and these amazing responses! (long, thoughtful pause) The responsiveness that one's own body felt and that the other person's body felt; I have never experienced such a passion, really. Such a passion that was *sustained* in a very physical way. It's very hard to describe, you know! I had felt very passionate with men in the past and had a lot of sexual experience, but this was something else. Two seconds and I was away!" (Virginia, 44)

This experience of sharing the same kind of body and the same sexual responses strongly reinforces both intimacy and erotic sensation. Clearly, no individual can 'know' that her partner feels 'the same' as she does, whether physically or emotionally, and women also need to learn about clitorises. There is no way to know how another person's orgasms or period pains feel in the 'real world'. Nevertheless, same-embodiment is experienced as very positive and pleasurable:

> "One of the biggest turn-ons for me is the fact that what I am touching, I am used to touching. I touch myself and I touch my partner and it feels like I have become two people and – all of that lovely fluidity! Being so physically intimate with a body so similar to mine is just extraordinary. I can't find the words for it. It really is!" (Adie, 29)

Although I have separated out these three elements – enjoyment of women's bodies, greater intimacy and the pleasures of physical sameness – they are interwoven in what women told me. Women who have spent a couple of decades or more as sexually active adults, and who are particularly well-placed to identify the differences between male and female lovers, tended to see it all as part of the same thing. Zara, who was 39 when we spoke, had found a joy and intensity with her girlfriend that she had looked for in vain throughout her married life, and it would be criminal to overanalyse the sheer poetry of her description:

> "She made my world sing. It was lovely being able to... Being very happy and very relaxed, being confirmed as to where I was... That I could have sex with another woman and get the pleasures that I never had with a man... The wonderful bit I always read about and I had expected when I had sex with my husband was that we would be entwined as an emotional thing and on a zingy level when we were actually together and having sex and climaxing and everything. It had never happened. And certainly, for me, I could feel it when she was close, I got electric feelings through me and it was absolutely great!" (Zara, 39)

Ah, but they were lesbians all along

At this point anyone who believes that lesbianism is something you are born with will be muttering that there are other reasons why the pleasure described by these women was so much greater than anything they had experienced with men. After all, if these women were 'really' lesbians all along, then of course they could hardly be expected to enjoy sex with men. In short, it is not that lesbian sex is in any way more pleasurable than heterosexual sex, it is simply that these women are somehow 'programmed' not to enjoy sex with men.

This misses the point. Firstly, everyone who has undertaken research into women's experiences of sex has come to the same conclusion, sex with men rarely lives up to women's expectations. This is such a commonly described phenomenon among heterosexual women that it has become the stuff of TV sitcoms, office jokes and stand-up comedy. Jokes about how long it takes a man to locate a clitoris, or about women faking orgasms, are commonplace. Clearly it is not just embryonic lesbians who find men sexually disappointing. Indeed, miserably unsatisfying sex with men is widely accepted to be the norm for the vast majority of the world's women. Professor Lesley Doyal, expert on women's health for the World Health Organisation, thinks the consequences of this common experience have been underestimated. "It is clear," she writes, "that coercive sex can be a significant cause of anxiety or depression. 'Routine' sex too may be an important but largely unrecognised element in the complex of factors that leave so many women with little sense of autonomy or self worth."[19]

A further point which makes it difficult to conclude that these women were 'born' lesbians who could never have enjoyed sex with men is that many interviewees were happy to acknowledge that their previous heterosexual partnerships had been good relationships with nice men. Thirty-nine-year-old Eve was particularly clear on this point; "When I got married it was a very happy day and, frankly, if I hadn't had these gay feelings I would still be with the guy now. A great life and a great bloke." She was not alone in stressing that her experiences of heterosexuality had been neither forced nor pretended. These are, quite clearly, not women who had been hiding the painful secret of their lesbianism and struggling to respond appropriately to men.

Many stated quite clearly that they *had* enjoyed sex with male partners, they just hadn't enjoyed it *as much* as sex with another woman. And it is when these women try to describe their experiences that we can start to pin down what exactly *are* the crucial differences between men and women as lovers. Tina who, at the age of 43, had plenty of experience to base her comparison on, was thoughtful:

> "I think, because I enjoy sex with a bloke as well, it can't just be sex. I think *emotionally* men and women are miles apart. What they want emotionally and, to a certain extent, affectionately, are so different." (Tina, 43)

And this does, indeed, seem to be the crux of the matter. The inability of many men to 'do' intimacy properly, their emotional inarticulacy and their detatched, formulaic approach to sex all seem to make it very difficult to enjoy sex with them. The two cannot successfully be separated, although Margaret did confess, "I am quite capable of enjoying sex with a man on a basic physical level, not on an emotional level."

The difference is beautifully summed up by Adie, who concludes, dryly:

> "I think it is the difference between the sexual *act*, which could be with man, woman or cucumber, and the feelings that go with it. For me, there are always feelings that go with it." (Adie, 29)

Conclusion? Lesbian sex is better for you!

For centuries, sex between women has been regarded as evil, sinful, wicked, deviant and bad for you. It is probably true to say that most of the world continues to think these things. But a careful examination of the evidence suggests something rather different. For starters, in purely physical terms, sex between two women is the safest kind of sex there is. No worries about pregnancy, no need to depend on contraceptives (most of which are bad for you in one way or another) and less chance of catching something unpleasant (it is, for example, difficult to transmit HIV during lesbian sex). Whilst recognising the damage caused to lesbians by stigma and discrimination, Lesley Doyal concludes, "Sex is still immeasurably safer between women than between women and men."[20]

It is not simply the safest kind of sex a woman can experience. In many societies where hostility towards homosexuality is decreasing, and where women have enough economic and social freedom to determine their own sexual lives, it is becoming clear that it may also be the most pleasurable sex a woman can experience. For the women in this study, who were well placed to reflect on the differences between men and women as sexual partners, lesbian sex was evidently a more pleasant and pleasurable experience – dramatically so for many of them.

This is wonderful for these women, and strong evidence against those who still want to stop women having sex with each other. It may also have wider implications in terms of lesbian wellbeing. Back to Professor Doyal on the consequences of 'routine' heterosex:

> "The negative consequences of being used as a means to the end of someone else's pleasure should not be underestimated, particularly when it is achieved through the very intimate act of bodily penetration. Moreover, many women also feel obliged to simulate sexual pleasure, thus exacerbating still further the alienation they may feel from their own body and their own senses."[21]

Perhaps now we can begin to understand why lesbian sexuality is well worth all the prejudice and discrimination. The scales may, indeed, be heavily weighted with insults, hostility and even violence. But what do we find in the other balance? Intimacy, beauty, desire, arousal, pleasure, self-esteem, joy, understanding and a way of being sexual which does not require us to lie back and think of England, to pretend a pleasure we do not feel, and to alienate ourselves from our bodies and our senses. Definitely worthwhile.

I would like to conclude this chapter with one final thought. The available evidence strongly suggests that lesbian sex is not only physically safer and enormously pleasurable but is positively good for women's mental and emotional wellbeing, in a way that sex with men generally fails to be. The evidence also suggests quite unambiguously that, given the miserable circumstances in which most of the world's women experience sex, this is a rare and precious thing. This being so, it becomes very difficult to imagine any sound ethical or moral reason why such a life-enhancing and health-promoting experience should be prohibited or regarded as less normal, right or proper than other kinds of sexual expression. Go, girls, go!

Watch out for guardian angels: Vikki and Jenny's story

Jenny and Vikki invited me to meet them in the house they share in southern England. Set in the tidy surroundings of an attractive estate with neatly clipped lawns and leafy gardens, their home welcomes visitors with light, sunny colours and a faint scent of fresh laundry. Both the wise side of 45, you would not give Vikki or Jenny a second glance if you passed one of them on the street. If, on the other hand, you were lucky enough to bump into both of them together, you could hardly fail to notice the chemistry between them. It is dazzling.

It was a baking hot day in early summer when I sat in their comfortable armchair sipping a reviving cup of tea. They sat together on the sofa opposite, clearly inseperable. They spoke as much to each other as to me, exchanging meaningful glances, sharing giggles and often drawing me with them into great howls of laughter. We all forgot about the tape recorder on the coffee table. When one was speaking about something difficult or painful, the other would touch her arm lightly or gently lean against her in silent support. They spoke together, presenting the one story from two perspectives. Here, in order to preserve the distinctness of their experiences (which were different in important ways, as they admit), I have transcribed each account separately.

Each recounted a story full of difficulty, frustration, pain and confusion. But that is not how they told it. For these two remarkable women, the joy of discovering that they loved each other, after a lifetime of being best friends, overshadows everything else. Listening to them gave me goosebumps, made my eyes fill up with tears, made me smile until my face hurt. Thank you, Vikki and Jenny, and I will let you tell it your way.

I started by asking them what word they would use to describe their sexuality. Jenny was quite definite, she liked 'gay'. Vikki, on the other hand, preferred 'lesbian'.

Vikki's side of the story

I don't mind 'lesbian', but I'd rather not be called a dyke, thank you! I lived a heterosexual life for quite a while, but I always had a nagging doubt. But it wasn't done; when I got married I was 21, and it wasn't something people did, to run off and live with a woman. So I tried to live that kind of life because it was the easiest way out. I left home and moved in with my nan, where I didn't have the opportunity to meet people as much, so I met my husband through a dating agency. It was Jen's idea.

Jen had got married and she had no idea how much I cared about her. I always knew that I cared for her quite a lot, so I thought, "Well, she's gone off and got married, so I'll go off and get married!", and she suggested joining a dating agency. I did, and I got married a year after I met him. But I have to be honest and say that I cared more for Jen than I cared for my husband! If she ever rang up in any kind of trouble, it wouldn't matter if dinner needed to be done or whatever, I would leave and go to her. Our relationship has always been the most important one.

There is a great song that goes, "Is that all there is?" That was my theme tune for twenty-odd years. I didn't really like myself until I decided who I was and should always have been. I would get up in the morning and really dislike myself, and I'd look in the mirror and pick pieces out of myself, and now I don't. It's not important any more what I look like, I am happy with who I am and I'm a much more confident person now.

It wasn't an unhappy marriage. I looked around for someone who had things in common with me. I would describe him as more like a brother. Someone who you could rely on. To be fair, he didn't want a lot anyway. He was not sexually over the top. He got his children, which is what he wanted, and he got his shirts ironed and his housework done and he was quite happy with all that. He wasn't really bothered about sex.

Well, I decided from quite a while back now that I was definitely a lesbian and I had to do something about it. But I had no idea how to go about it or what to do! I was totally convinced that Jen wasn't interested in me in that way and that we were just really good friends. Then three or four things happened. I had an operation, got thrombosis and nearly died and I thought, "God, if I had died without knowing who I was, this is more awful than finding out I am a lesbian!" Then Princess Diana died and I realised anyone can die at any age, and I was still sitting here, hating myself and not knowing who I really am.

Then I started a new job, and I got on quite well with one of the girls at work, and I found out that she was a lesbian. She was a lot younger than me, but really nice, and I decided that I needed to ask her how to go about this. I wasn't interested in her as a partner, but I thought that she might just be able to point me in the right direction. So, since I tell Jen everything, I sat down and told her one night. I said, "Sarah at work is a lesbian, and I'm going to meet her outside of work, because I think this is who I am and I'm going to lay my cards on the table and tell her. Because I'd like to know how to go about coming out."

Jen said, "No, no, you're not. You've got a husband. Don't be silly!" We had a lot of conversations about it for a couple of days. Then she phoned me and said, "Look, if I ask you not to go and meet Sarah, would you not go?" I thought she was persuading me not to, so I said, "No Jen, I'm going. But I will come and see you first." So I drove down to see her, and she said she was in love with me.

I couldn't stop my heart racing. It was the best thing that had ever happened to me, because it was something I had wanted for twenty-odd years. I couldn't believe it. I thought, "God, she's finally said it, this is wonderful!" Then I asked her if I could kiss her. The stupid thing is that we talked, and I said, "I can't leave Ronan and the kids," and Jen said, "Well, I'm not leaving Derek." We had no idea what to do. That was November

25th and, from then up until New Year's Eve we did just see each other when we could.

We used to ring each other every day. All the time we were married and didn't know how each other felt, we would ring each other once a week. I'd ring Jen one week, she'd ring me the next. But now, we'd ring each other every day, before we went to work, any time we could. Then it all got taken out of our hands.

My husband is a shift worker, and he was working on New Year's Eve. So myself and my youngest daughter went to Jen and Derek's to celebrate New Year. I got slightly tipsy, which probably didn't help, and Jen was driving because we had to go and pick my daughter up from a party she'd been to. We had had a meal, and some drinks, and Jen stayed sober to drive. We left much earlier than we needed to pick her up, just to have some time together. Then we brought her back, and we engineered it that everyone else went to bed and Jenny and I just stayed up for quite a long time. The next day, once my daughter and I had left, Derek asked Jen what was going on.

When Derek told her he knew, she rang up and said, "What am I going to do? He wants me to leave." I went downstairs and my husband asked what was going on, and I told him, "Jen and Derek are splitting up and I want to go with Jen, because I love her." At first he thought it was his fault, because he didn't want sex any more than I did, and he offered to go to a counsellor and sort out his problems. Then he looked at me and said, "But that's not what you want, is it?" I said, "No, I want to be with Jen, and we will move out when we find somewhere we can go."

So, every time he was on nights he would let Jen come round and we would sleep in our bed. I had to sleep with him still, because we didn't have anywhere else for me to go. He's a funny person; he was quite happy to stay in the same bed and to let Jen come round when he was on nights, as long as he didn't see her. It was the most weird thing we were doing. Derek wouldn't go anywhere near Jen. He still cooked her meals: he would always get in before her so he'd still cook her a meal if she was coming home. But every time her husband was on nights, Jen would come around and stay. She would have to make sure she was in the study when he came home, getting dressed, so she could leave once he had gone to bed. It sounds stupid now, doesn't it? But this is what we were doing!

Ronan was exceptionally dependent on me. But he's changed since I left. It was difficult, but it sounds more unreal now talking about it. It got to the stage where we actually spent a couple of nights in Travelodges when we were trying to sort everything out. Derek was really pressuring Jen to leave and if we didn't go to the Travelodge we ended up just driving round the countryside in the car, ending up sitting in car parks. At 44 and 46 it's strange to sit snogging in a car park (which is all we ever did) – we're still learning what sex is. So we would end up booking Travelodges now and then, just to get away.

But I felt, this is what has been missing in my life. I do believe I was born gay. I kept going – not exactly a string of fellows, but one after the other, trying to find what I couldn't find because I was with the wrong sex. I had been with a few men, simply trying to find this thrill which I get with Jen that was eluding me. I watched lots of television programmes because I was searching for myself and I thought that they would help me. Funnily enough, the [gay] programmes seem to have dried up lately; there used to be more on the telly than there are now. There was quite a good series, which I used to watch. I wanted Jen to watch them, but they don't seem to be on any more. I watched them trying to find out whether that seemed to be the right thing for me, trying to recognise something.

I went about it all very consciously for three or four years, but not knowing where to go for that final push, until Sarah at work said to me, "I'm a lesbian." Then it suddenly hit me that maybe this was my chance. It was almost like somebody had sent her there. My guardian angel, someone sent to free me from what I didn't want to be.

Now Jen and I have opened up to each other and there are hundreds of things we can think of. Jen said the day she got married I turned up really late, because I knew I didn't want her to get married. It was the hardest thing I had ever done, having to go there and see her getting married. She says she kept wondering where I was; I was the only person she really wanted to see there. It never dawned on her then, but now you can put it into the context of what should have been!

We are fortunate that none of our friends have turned their backs on us. They come around. But it's not the same, because you can sit there, and they sympathise with you, but there are things we can't talk to them about. You can't really say how much you care for each other. We can touch each other, but you have to respect other people's wishes.

Sometimes you feel very isolated, because you just want to meet those other people that are like you.

I'm very lucky at work. Not only is there Sarah, there is also another lesbian at work. I've been lucky enough, without ramming it down people's throats, to be open about it. So everybody I work with knows my situation, to the extent that we have actually been invited to a wedding in a couple of weeks' time. I was really chuffed with that. To actually be invited out as a couple.

Jenny's side of the story

I like the word 'gay'. I've always thought 'lesbian' was such an awful word, I don't know why. But I have not always been gay, definitely not! I've always felt that I had attractions to other women, and I used to think it was because I just liked them. Whenever I met new people, through my job or whatever, and got on with them very well indeed, I used to feel a sort of underlying attraction, but I didn't know it at the time. I suppose I swept it under the carpet. But I used to become obsessed with these people. I would focus on them terribly, and I think my husband used to get a bit concerned! It wasn't everybody, just certain women that I met. Not men. Though I would look at a man and think, "Well, he is quite nice looking." I had always liked rugged types.

I was living a heterosexual life. I was with my husband Derek for 28 years. I was 22 when we married, and I'd known him since I was 16 and he was 17. He was like my best friend. I did love him, in my own way, but not as I love Vik... Very different!

My relationship with her has always been my most important relationship. If either one of us was in trouble, we would just drop everything and go and help each other. Derek thought that was just because we were best friends, but something cropped up only a few months after we were married. Vikki was ill, and I sat up with her all night, virtually. When I think about it, when you're newlyweds you don't leave your husband to go and sit with your best mate!

Everybody expects you to get married and have children and I went along with the flow. I wouldn't have swapped any of my life with Derek, because we had a happy married life. The only thing lacking was the sex. I never enjoyed having sex with a man whatsoever. Never, never. I thought it was because I didn't have a very high sex drive and I just had to put up with it. But that was the only thing. We got on exceptionally well together. I always knew something was missing, but I could never put my finger on it (if I can use that term!). So it was a bit of a shock when it all happened...

My husband had a very high sex drive, and I'm certain I couldn't satisfy him. I think he just got to the stage where he would think, "Oh well, this is better than nothing." It was terribly, terribly difficult, I used to think, "Surely I should be feeling a bit more than this?" I didn't want to hurt him, but there wasn't much I could do about it. But, oh god! It's different now. Quite amazing!

How did Vik and I get together? Well, I had been off work with a back problem and I had a lot of time to sit at home and think and it just hit me. I thought, "My god, I love her!" Don't ask me what time of day it was or whatever, I can't tell you, but it was just the most peculiar sensation and then I kept thinking to myself, "No, this is ridiculous, don't be ridiculous, Jen! You've known Vik nearly 29 years, she's your best mate, don't be ridiculous." But I just couldn't get it out of my head.

This was the first time it had ever happened to me. I think when we first met I had felt an attraction to her but, because we were a lot younger then, I thought it was just stupid. I remembered that, when I was twelve, I used to go and stay with my godparents in the summer and there was this girl who lived next door. I just always wanted to be near her, next to her, and I really liked her. I told my godmother this and she said, "That happens, dear, when you are growing up." So I thought these feelings that I had for Vik... Perhaps something like that was happening! Then this one day I just sat down and thought, "My god, I'm really in love with her," and it frightened the life out of me.

I kept thinking first, "Well, I have to tell her," and then, "No! I won't tell her," and this kept going on and on. I was really in turmoil about what on earth to do. Here's me, married nearly 25 years; it's not been awful and I wasn't unhappy. But this feeling was getting stronger and stronger throughout the day, and all of a sudden I just picked up the phone and said, "You have got to come and see me!" She said, "Oh, all right then, but I am going to go out with this Sarah first."

I just told her. I just leant across to her and, how I had the guts to do it I don't know; I said, "You really need to know, I am in love with you." I was shaking by that time, and we were both shaking and clinging on to each other. My husband was just in the next room, the study, and I thought, "My god, he won't know what's going on!" He was used to me and Vik being together, but there's him in there and we're in here, and we were clinging on to each other for dear life! It was a most peculiar sensation, but I felt this wave of pure relief come over me when I told her.

It sounds awful, really, a bit Mills & Boon! When she said to me, "Can I kiss you?" I thought, "Oooh! I've got to kiss a woman!" I felt rather strange about that, but after we had kissed I didn't find it a bit awkward, and we've carried on kissing ever since!

We were really shaking; I suppose it was mixed emotions. It seems like yesterday, but it was most peculiar. She was saying, "I don't want to leave," and I said, "You've got to go, you've got to go back to Ronan and the kids." We thought we were going to carry on some sordid affair, I think!

But it felt so different from with my husband. My god, yes! Extremely exciting. I couldn't wait to see her again. And I had never been in love with anybody in my life before. If this is real love then, yes, thank you! It just hit us like a bombshell and it still does. Hopefully you can see we are very much in love and it just gets better every day.

But that New Year, Derek asked me what was going on. He's a very intuitive man. So I didn't deny it. I just said, "Yes." From then on it got horrible, I'm afraid. As it would do. He burst into tears, and so did I, and I moved straight into the spare room and that was me, done and dusted; we've never even discussed it really. My husband is a man who used to put everything in boxes, that's just how he is. We even had a ceremony where he took off his wedding ring in front of me, that was awful. He cut up the credit cards in front of me, and it went on from there.

But for some reason, I don't know why, I felt I could handle him. I felt a complete inner strength, and for the first time in my life I could handle him. He was a very likeable person, but he had always dominated because when we met I was very shy. Though I did get him to go to teacher training because I felt that he was being wasted in the job that he was doing; so I kept him for four years. He's turned out to be a marvellous teacher. I did it because I wanted to do it; I didn't find it a hardship. I felt that there was a man with a talent and it was wasted. So, oh my god! It was awful! It still is because at least Vik's husband has sat down and talked about it, whereas Derek really hasn't.

But I do feel that Ronan would have allowed us to go along as we were just to keep her there. I don't think it's because he loved Vikki; it was the fact that he was losing someone who had waited on him hand and foot, because that's what she did. She was like their little matriarch, running round after him and the kids. Whereas in my marriage we helped each other. We were dealing with two men who were completely different, even when we used to go out in a foursome.

I couldn't believe how I felt about Vikki! I have never felt this elated about anything in my life. I thought, "Do I really deserve to have these feelings, after living with a man all these years?" But I found it wonderfully exciting, and I still do. It gets more exciting by the minute! But very scary at the same time, because here I am, I'm 48 now, and I think, "God, I've had to wait until I was 47 before I've ever had these feelings in my life!" But I love it, and I wouldn't swap a single moment of it.

I have tried to look at this from all sorts of angles. How did I get these feelings and why has whoever made us decided that I should be gay? All I know is that it is the most wonderful feeling I have ever experienced and, whoever gave that to me, well, thanks very much! I'm just very sorry that it's taken me all this time to get here, but it's even more marvellous to think that I've known her for nearly thirty years and now we are a couple! I don't think there are many people who can say that.

We've discussed these things a lot. On my wedding day everybody else was more exhilarated than me. All I could think of was, "Where's Vik?" We had always enjoyed each other's company, and we always used to prefer going out on our own, rather than in a foursome with our husbands, because we could be ourselves. We were just like kids. We used to go up to Oxford Street every Thursday, and we used to play in shop doorways. We were like big kids, but we had so much fun!

There must be so many people out there in the same boat, and we would really like to meet some of those people! That's what we are desperate to do, because we don't really have much of a social life. When I was married I was always going out. I used to play bowls. I found it a bit boring, but I've got a few cups to prove it.

My friends have become friends of ours. But the only thing is, their other halves haven't always. I have got one friend whose husband doesn't want to know. But you don't want to embarrass people; some people may not be able to handle it. There are only two people at work who know. I don't go around saying, "Hi, I've been in a marriage for 25 years and I'm gay!" I have done it very carefully. I have picked the people out that I thought would be OK, and I was right. Everybody still talks about fellas to me, and I join in with all of that, about the size of so-and-so's whatsit! I would love to stand up and make an announcement, but I don't think that's the right thing for me to do. I want to tell them how much I love her. I suppose that will all come in time. If she was a bloke I could invite them to the wedding.

Notes

1. In 1982, Lord Justice Watkins gave it as his legal opinion that "if a parent becomes homosexual after a marital breakdown the courts should not allow children to be brought up in a homosexual household... and should only consider awarding custody... to the homosexual parent if there is clearly no acceptable alternative." (*Capital Gay* no. 53, 23 July 1982)
2. See Angela Mason & Anya Palmer, *Queer Bashing: A national survey of hate crimes against lesbians and gay men*, Stonewall, London, 1996.
3. See Tamsin Wilton & Carly Hall, *Second Best Value: Lesbian, gay and bisexual life in Bristol*, Bristol City Council Equalities Unit, 1999.
4. See Debbie Epstein, *Challenging Lesbian and Gay Inequalities in Education*, Open University Press, Buckingham, 1994.
5. See Tamsin Wilton & Lori Streich, *A Local Catch 22 Situation: A survey of lesbian, gay and bisexual life in South Gloucestershire*, South Gloucestershire Equalities Unit, 2002.
6. See Dale Spender, *Man Made Language* (2nd edn), Routledge & Kegan Paul, New York, 1985.
7. See Sheila Jeffreys, *AntiClimax: A feminist perspective on the sexual revolution*, The Women's Press, London, 1990.
8. Ibid.
9. Germaine Greer, *The Female Eunuch*, Granada, London, 1970.
10. Shere Hite, *Women and Love: A cultural revolution in progress*, Penguin, Harmondsworth, 1987.
11. Interview by Angela Hamblin, 'Is a feminist heterosexuality possible?' in Sue Cartledge and Joanna Ryan, *Sex and Love: New thoughts on old contradictions*, London, The Women's Press, 1983.

12. Margaret Nichols, 'Lesbian sexuality: Issues and developing theory', in Boston Lesbian Psychologies Collective (eds), Lesbian Psychologies, University of Illinois Press, Chicago, 1987.
13. Lillian Faderman, *Surpassing the Love of Men: Romantic friendship and love between women from the Renaissance to the present*, The Women's Press, London, 1985.
14. See Sheila Jeffreys, *The Lesbian Heresy*, Spinifex Press, Melbourne, 1993.
15. Leeds Revolutionary Feminists pamphlet, reprinted in *Love Your Enemy? The debate between heterosexual feminism and political lesbianism*, edited and published by Onlywomen Press, London, 1981.
16. Ibid.
17. Mary Calderone & Eric Johnson, *The Family Book about Sexuality*, Harper & Row, London, 1989.
18. With apologies to Alan Partridge.
19. Lesley Doyal, *What Makes Women Sick: Gender and the political economy of health* London, Macmillan, 1995.
20. Ibid.
21. Ibid.

3

WHAT SHALL WE TELL THE CHILDREN?

"I resent the fact that I've got to hide it from their friends. In the beginning, I was paranoid about letting them have friends for tea or to stay. That's changed, because of their attitudes, I think. Because they are, like, 'Well, if anybody says anything to me, I will tell them, What's wrong with it? She's my mum. If you don't like it, you are not my friend.' I'm proud that they can be proud of me, but I do resent the fact that they've got to know about the bad things." (Charlotte, 30)

For many people the very idea of a lesbian mother is a contradiction in terms. Mums, after all, are supposed to be everything that lesbians are not. 'Mum' is about normality, stability, security and self-sacrifice. Perhaps above all, it is *not* about sex and sexuality. Mothering is such a physically intimate business that there is a great deal of cultural anxiety about the sexuality of mothers. 'Lesbian', on the other hand, is loaded down with negative meanings about being abnormal, unstable, neurotic and even unnatural.

Notions about nature and naturalness are particularly powerful when it comes to sex. Even the most tolerant heterosexuals may take it for granted that homosexuality is 'unnatural'. Well, they may argue, you don't find animals doing it, do you? And if nature had *intended* us to be gay, the species would become extinct, wouldn't it? This from people who are probably quite happy to take part in such unnatural activities as smoking cigarettes, flying in aeroplanes or shaving their legs!

This belief that homosexuality is unnatural is not, in fact, supported by the evidence. Animal studies have shown, quite conclusively, that individuals of many species *do* form same-sex pairs or engage in same-sex sex play.[1] Moreover, such behaviour is often observed when there is no shortage of 'opposite sex' mates available and some same-sex pair-bonding is life-long. I offer this information since it can sometimes provide useful ammunition in arguments with ill-informed friends and family members, but we should really be asking, what *is* 'natural' exactly? When it comes to sex, we like to kid ourselves that we are doing what comes naturally, but in fact our sexual behaviour is *more* rule-bound and governed by social convention than anything else we do.

In the teeth of every scrap of evidence, however, many people continue to believe that women's biological sex drive is programmed in the interests of species reproduction. In short, women 'naturally' want babies. Of course, women cannot make each other pregnant. So, runs the argument, if there is nothing 'more natural' than a woman wanting to have children, then there is nothing at all 'natural' about her preferring to have sexual relationships with other women. Even worse, while 'normal' women gladly sacrifice their own happiness in order to have babies and bring them up, lesbians are (selfishly and unnaturally) interested in their own sexual pleasure. Within the terms of this particular story, a lesbian mother who leaves her marriage is breaking all the rules of motherhood. If she goes so far as to leave her own children behind and move out with a woman lover, she risks being seen as utterly thoughtless and immoral.

We could argue until the cows came home about whether women's desire for children is instinctive or produced by social conditioning. This argument is impossible to resolve, and it really doesn't matter. The point is that for many women, the longing to have children feels very powerful. These longings, combined with social assumptions and the pressure to live in reproductive family groups, have important implications for lesbians. They mean, for example, that plenty of new lesbians are mothers bringing up children when they come out. As we shall see, this is something that the lesbian community is not particularly well-equipped to deal with.

Lesbian motherhood can be an intensely challenging experience, as 35-year-old Theresa found. As she explained, "I was brought up Italian, Catholic, just no question from a very young age. I had linen bought for me for when I got married, from the age of six, seven years old." Having obediently followed the script that had been laid down for her, how did she experience the realisation that she was a lesbian? "Oh, it was devastating, because I was married with children." As for so many of the women in this chapter, it was a recognition that was to throw her life into confusion.

I thought the only way I could have kids would be with a man

The longing for children can draw women very strongly towards heterosexuality. After all, the family story that we all grow up with is about Mummy, Daddy and a variable number of kids. Women told me that this had been an unquestioned goal for them. Some of the older women commented that the younger generation has choices that they did not. For 50-year-old Jodie, leaving her husband when she found herself pregnant was simply not an option. It was to cost her her first lesbian partner:

> "She wanted me to leave and have the baby with her, but I said no, because I was brought up to believe children are brought up with a mummy and a daddy. It was as simple as that... I did want to have children. If I was 20 now, I would seriously think that I could have a family with a woman." (Jodie, 50)

Things are never simple, however, and even some younger women find it hard to let go of the notion that children come along with heterosexuality:

> "I think the reason I [thought I should have relationships with men] was very much wrapped up in the children thing. I thought the only way that I could have kids would be with a man. Now I think, well, yes, I do, that is something that I want, but I'm not necessarily going to be doing that with a man as my partner." (Kate, 26)

The assumption that only heterosexuals are equipped to have children can also make it more difficult for parents to accept their daughter's lesbian life. Julie, who was 35 when we spoke, explained, "My mum had a sense of loss about whether I would ever have children and grandchildren, and all of the conventional life." This sense of lost opportunity can hit some parents really hard. Of course, increasing numbers of non-lesbian women are deciding not to have children, but this is of little comfort to deprived would-be grandparents!

If wanting children can draw women towards heterosexuality, being a mother can act to keep them in heterosexual relationships and marriages. This can result in tremendously stressful and painful situations, where women feel torn in two. It is important to understand the reasons why this can be so difficult. Not all mothers are alike, and every relationship between a mother and child is unique. Yet most would agree that being a mother is not like any other kind of relationship. Not only do you experience powerful feelings of love, but in addition there comes a responsibility like no other. Mothers are, after all, responsible for keeping their children alive. Moreover, so significant is the bond between mother and child (socially, culturally and psychologically) that women continue to feel an enormous responsibility for their children's wellbeing long after they have ceased to be physically dependent.

For many women there is the additional problem of financial independence. A woman who has always thought of herself first and foremost as a wife and mother may never have done paid work. Even for women who do work as a matter of course, many jobs traditionally done by conventionally married women pay very little and tend to be part-time with few promotion prospects. Working at a supermarket checkout may fit in wonderfully with school hours, but it isn't likely to offer enough money to support a family.

In such circumstances, it is hardly surprising that some women reach an uncomfortable compromise. They may try to find ways of maintaining a lesbian relationship whilst remaining in a marriage:

> "In practical terms it's very difficult because, basically, I'm not prepared to consider leaving [my husband] and I've got a seven-year-old. It's simply a matter of practicalities and finding someone who is prepared to take the very little amount of attention that I would be prepared to give them." (Louise, 30)

However determined women may be to stick doggedly at an emotionally empty marriage until their children have grown up and left home, the strain can prove intolerable:

> "I left my husband when I was 40; 'life begins' and all that. So I was actually in the relationship with him for about ten years and quite deliberately deciding to do nothing about being a lesbian at all. My thought process was, my daughter has got to come first, she is more important than all that sort of stuff. And then it just got intolerable and I left." (Elizabeth, 45)

Others are able to keep going long enough to see their children grow up to an age where they seem more able to handle such a dramatic transformation in their mother's life. Margaret had been quite extraordinarily strong and determined, and had somehow even managed to organise her life well enough to ensure that she was able to support herself financially once she took the final step:

> "I divorced my husband four years ago, after a long marriage – 23 years of misery. Two children, fitting in with society, doing the right thing. And then I thought, no! I just couldn't bear it any longer. I just couldn't see

> myself doing this until I was in my 50s and 60s and retiring with this man. No, I am not going to do it any more. I was late coming into nursing, and I split up with him as soon as I qualified. As soon as I was able to financially support myself, and my children were that much older, I called it a day." (Margaret, 46)

With the best will in the world, however, women struggling on in such difficult circumstances may find that lesbian love takes them by surprise! Sometimes the woman of your dreams just turns up, and everything shifts:

> "I made the decision to think, well, OK, I will be with my children until they are old enough to look after themselves and then I will find out for myself [if I am a lesbian]. I sort of made this decision anyway, so I didn't expect to find anybody *now* in my life, because obviously I was going to look after my children first. It was a total surprise! It was very scary, actually, at the time." (May, 39)

So, having children can act as a barrier to women who are trying to find ways of expressing or exploring their lesbian feelings. On the other hand, it can bring women into contact with unexpected lesbian possibilities. Many 'ordinary' women who have never dreamed of questioning their heterosexuality, meet their first lesbian love at the school gate, at playgroup or taking their children swimming. This is, quite simply, because the labour market is organised in such a way that most of those who work with children are women. Mothers of young children tend to inhabit a world largely populated with other women. Although the presence of 'new' (or unemployed) men with babies and young children has become more noticeable in the last decade or so, they remain the exception rather than the rule.

This may go some way to explain one of the unexpected findings of my research; the numbers of women – and they were almost always mothers – who fell in love with their best friend. It also explains why many unsuspecting women found themselves seized with lesbian desire in the most unlikely places and for the most unlikely women:

> "It all happened by accident. I was very unhappily married and I had suddenly developed a massive crush on my son's teacher, which was awful, because I didn't know what to do. Obviously, I wasn't going to do anything about her, but I realised that I had started to feel very out of control, and there wasn't anybody I could talk to, anybody I could tell." (Catherine, 40)

Lesley who, at 30, was the mother of five young children, fell in love quite unexpectedly with a woman while her husband was serving a prison sentence. "I started taking my kids to a summer play centre," she recalls, "and just met someone there." Still very fond of her husband, she couldn't bring herself to tell him while he was stuck in prison, so found herself in the difficult position of trying to come to terms with the unfamiliar new identity – 'lesbian' – while continuing to visit and support him as best she could.

Your mum's a lesbian!

For women who come out and have to deal with the impact on their marriages and children, there are many things to consider and much emotional trauma to manage. Apart from anything else, it can be extremely difficult for the 'new' lesbian mother's partner, perhaps particularly if she herself does not have children. If she has been living as a lesbian for a long time, she may not have much experience with children or with mothers (other than her own). It is likely to be especially challenging if she suddenly finds herself having to deal with a relationship that has a man in it. Most mothers are concerned to protect their children's relationship with their father, and this means that contact – often in fraught or unhappy circumstances – between him and his ex-wife's lesbian lover is unavoidable. This can spark off all sorts of insecurities:

> "... She found it too awkward a situation, and she still does. When [my ex-husband] comes to pick up the children, she does find that a bit difficult. She was very insecure about the fact that I was straight, frightened that I would go back. There is no way, no way. I wish I could stop her feeling insecure, but I know that I can't." (Charlotte, 30)

In lesbian relationships where one woman has children and the other doesn't, there are different issues for both women. If the childless lesbian is unfamiliar with children (and, of course, having no children of your own does not necessarily mean you are unaccustomed to them), this can be stressful for everyone involved. She remains, however, the more free of the two women. If she decides to leave the relationship, she leaves the mother to deal with the fallout for her children, and her greater independence can seem both enviable and threatening.

> "I remember, I was so devastated when she left me, it was after six years and I thought it would be for ever. But she just turned up and said, can I have the money you owe me for the shopping, I have decided you are not giving me what I want, I have decided to leave. And I was stunned. So off she went, and there was nothing I could do, because my son, he was twelve at the time, he was asleep upstairs and I was trying to cry quietly so as not to wake him, when what I wanted to do was just howl and howl. I couldn't cope at all, so I phoned the London Lesbian and Gay Switchboard, and I got this gay man. And he was really, really out of his depth. I was just sobbing and crying down the phone at him and saying, how could she do that, how could she just walk in here and say that, after six years. And so he said, why don't

> you go after her and try to talk to her, and I said I can't, I'm stuck in the house, I've got my son asleep upstairs and you don't just leave the house with a child asleep in it. And he couldn't understand why I couldn't leave my son asleep in the house on his own, and somehow that was worst of all, that I was trapped. And I asked her, have you thought what this is going to do to him? Because he adored her, she was like his second mum and we were his family. And she said, no, to be quite honest, I never thought about it. After six years, she didn't think about what it would do to him at all." (Sally, 47)

It is, of course, understandable that women who do not have children, and may never have wanted to have children, might find it a struggle to remain committed to a relationship with a mother. For many reasons, the children's needs have to come first, and it may be a new and difficult experience not to be the most important person in your lover's life. But the woman who decides that she can't handle it and walks out may leave great heartache behind her. The mother who has been left in such circumstances may feel very abandoned:

> "My last girlfriend I felt very upset with because we parted and I feel that, because she is 32, she is a professional, she's been a lesbian all her life, she has got no ties, she has money, her life's totally different to me. All this, 'I love you blah blah blah,' but she couldn't support me! I wasn't asking her to live with me and be involved in the children's lives or anything, but she had to step out because she couldn't take the pressure of the fact that I'm going to court with the children's father... I felt it was very selfish of her, though I will always be grateful for the time and attention that she paid to me to enable me to feel what I have felt. But it's also very difficult, because I have so much guilt, because I have my children and, obviously I am a mother and my children have to come first. You know that, but when you want...

> I want something for myself now. I have spent my whole life not getting anything, not wanting, and now I am finding things hard to cope with, because now I really want for myself." (Lesley, 30)

A different kind of hearbreak confronts those women who, for whatever reason, have to leave their children behind when they move out of the family home. Of course, heterosexual women do this too, but there is undoubtedly added guilt and stigma for those women who leave their children and go off to live as lesbians. For some, it all feels too painful to endure, and the pull to return can be very hard to resist. Jill's girlfriend was very closeted and unwilling to sign up for a committed relationship with her. In consequence, she found it enormously difficult to convince herself that she was doing the right thing:

> "My son... I think I've done a lot of harm to him in leaving him. I'm trying to put that right. He is the most important person in the universe to me... The only reason I want to be back with my husband is because of our background together and because of my son." (Jill, 51)

In this unhappy situation, Jill found herself painfully torn in two directions. I often wonder how she resolved her dilemma.

When April left her family, in her early 40s, to live openly as a lesbian, she took nothing with her but her savings. With nowhere to live and no idea how long it might take her to establish her new life, she did not feel able to tear her child away from the security and stability of home life with their father. She talks about it quietly, without drama, but it clearly upsets her:

> "I just couldn't take her with me. I had £4,000 and I didn't have anywhere to live and I didn't know what the future was going to hold, so I had to leave her where she was. Now she is settled into school and everything, and even though there is a spare room and my girlfriend

> would be fine about having her to stay with us, she doesn't come. I can't force her." (April, 45)

Fortunately, increasing social tolerance towards lesbians means there is more acceptance of lesbian mothers than at any time in the past. Crucially, family courts are now unlikely to decide that being a lesbian automatically makes a woman an unfit mother.[2] It is also true that greater equality between the sexes means that women are more able to find work that pays enough to live on than their mothers and grandmothers ever were. Of course, having responsibility for young children drastically reduces the job opportunities open to you, and mothers who have uprooted their children may have good reason to spend as much time with them as possible. This may further limit their choices in terms of paid work. Nevertheless, it is becoming increasingly rare for women to have to lose their children when they come out.

Of course, things are very different again when both women have children. I spoke to several women who found themselves leaving conventional marriages and nuclear families and setting up quite large 'blended' families with another mother and *her* children. This was the commonest outcome when women fell in love with a best friend. Ann and George ended up with six children between them and their obviously happy new life seems to fascinate everyone in the quiet country town where they live. As Ann tells it:

> "We made friends through our children. She was a swimming teacher and I used to go and, of all the people, sat at the side of the pool... And I go to the Pony Club with the Pony Club mothers, and my children are everywhere... [And now] we bicker on the side of the pool like a married couple, and that makes them laugh!" (Ann, 37)

But however happy the relationship, and whatever the circumstances that the adults find themselves in, newly out lesbians living with children all face the same burning question, what do we tell the children?

Mummy's got something important to tell you

Telling your children that you are a lesbian is not the sort of thing covered in most parenting handbooks. Yet it can be one of the most troubling steps a mother has to take. As one mother put it, "Gay is also having to tell my children and worrying that it's a big thing for them to accept, that they have got a gay mum." There are anxieties about how to ensure emotional support for the child, both within the family and in the outside world. The first concern is about the mother–child relationship and, in many cases, about the complexities of the mother–father–child triangle. Mothers worry that hurt and angry male partners may use their lesbianism against them, or that negative social attitudes will affect their kids, making a child hostile or fearful towards its mother. This is a heartbreaking prospect for any mother, and comes along with deep-seated fears about the possible impact on the child's emotional wellbeing. Even where such fears prove groundless, there is always the lurking dread that emotional problems will appear later on in the child's life. Such fears prevent some women from telling their children altogether:

> "There are times when I really want to tell someone. It's like, my daughter and her friend, their latest insult is 'gay'. But it doesn't mean *gay*. If somebody is wearing a dress that's really horrible, or playing some music they don't like, they say, 'Oh, that's really gay!' She is about 25 and is very 'Well, I have been to university and I have got lots of way-out friends, and I am funky and with it.' But, the shock, to hear it from her mother! Sometimes I would really like to tell them, to see what would happen, but it can't be done." (Barbara, 49)

Despite such fears, mothers generally found that their children responded well to the information. When this happened, it was both reassuring and thrilling:

> "My kids' attitudes are important to me. They are absolutely amazing. They are ten, eight and almost

seven. They are just amazing. I feel proud of the way I have brought them up. They have got no discrimination towards anybody at all. I haven't actually come out to my son and said, I'm gay. He knows Deb lives here, and he knows we sleep in the same bed, but I haven't used any labels for him and he just accepts it all for what it is. My girls, they know the labels. My oldest more so than my middle one. She doesn't like the labels. She knows they are there but she doesn't like them. I'm just Mum, and Deb's Deb. When I told her she was, like, well, as long as you're happy, Mum, I'm happy." (Charlotte, 30)

This is not easy information for children to deal with and they react in many different ways. Sometimes a son seems to find it easier than a daughter and sometimes vice versa. Younger children seem to find it much easier to accept than older children, who may already have been exposed to more negative social attitudes. For one ten-year-old girl, there didn't seem to be anything to make a fuss about:

> "My daughter, she accepts it. She knows I was with her dad and that I am now with my partner. She doesn't know anything different. She is ten years of age. She is very open-minded, you can tell her anything." (Michelle, 30)

As with so much else, it is adolescent children who may find things much more challenging. They are becoming aware of sexuality themselves, and more strongly influenced by the opinions of their peers:

> "My daughter [16] was quite upset at first because she has had a lot of problems herself at school in the past with bullying, but she did say to me, 'I'm not bothered about that, Mum, it's other people's reactions that I am bothered about,' and it was really emotional when I talked to her about it. But, saying that, she gets on really

> well with my partner and she is in counselling herself. She talked to the counsellor and that seemed to be really helpful. My son is 14. I actually came out to him a couple of months back. And it was really traumatic because at first he was supposed to be staying the night here, and he wouldn't stay. He said, 'I'm going back to my dad.' I got really upset, and he said, 'I still love you, Mum, I've just got to get used to it.' So he rang me up later on that night, and he was really angry and said, 'You should never have got married or had kids.' And that's what my daughter said to me, too. I just said, 'Well, it's all right to say that but there are a lot of people who are in my position and that's the way it worked out. I know it's hard to understand.' I was really upset because [my son] said to me, 'I don't want to know you, I don't want to speak to you again.' So I was really upset that night. But he rang me the next morning, obviously he had had time to think. He said, 'I'm sorry Mum, I still love you. It doesn't matter whether it's a man or a woman that you love, it just doesn't matter. It's the person you are that counts.' So I was really proud of him for that, for a 14-year-old." (Liz, 42)

Clearly, Liz's son had been landed with this shocking new information and had taken himself off to be alone and wrestle with it as best he could, leaving her on an emotional roller-coaster ride. No wonder she is so proud of his ability to take it on board and deal with it in less than 24 hours! It was, not surprisingly, a common experience that children just needed time to process this new knowledge about their mother. It is also very important to leave them the space and independence to fit it into their own lives in a way that makes sense for them. "My daughter was, I think, upset to begin with," explained 44-year-old Jane, "She didn't know what to do, but she has come to terms with it and she is good about it. She's 21, and still finds it a bit difficult. I don't know who she tells and who she doesn't, that's up to her."

Sometimes, the news comes as no surprise to children, who may already have worked things out for themselves. If this happens, the process of adjustment will have begun. What such children need most urgently is honesty from the adults concerned, and a matter-of-fact willingness to answer their questions:

> "My daughter found out about me before anyone else, my youngest one, the twelve-year-old. She came down to see me and she said, 'Mum, are you going to be a lesbian?' She was only eleven. She understood, she knew what was going on well before anybody else had any idea. That was because she was a nosy child. She would look in my drawers and places I had hidden [lesbian] books and things like that. Nobody else looked in there, but of course she did, and unfortunately she found out.
>
> "She seems to be fine. She is an absolute star, she just takes everything in her stride. If I do talk to my other children, the older ones, and I ask how they think she is, they say, 'She is fine, Mum.' She just gets on with her life and that's it.'" (April, 45)

Even for children who work this out for themselves, it can still be an extremely difficult thing to come to terms with. If their mother's new lesbian identity enters their lives along with traumatic events like family breakup or the loss of one or other parent, it is not surprising that it can take a long time for them to feel safe enough to be accepting. Children whose parents separate often give vent to powerful feelings of anger and unhappiness, and this can be very difficult indeed for their parents. For lesbian mothers it can be particularly upsetting and may cause terrible feelings of guilt. It is important to remember that family breakup is a big thing for *all* children to handle, not only the children of lesbian mothers! For Elizabeth, who had to leave her daughter behind when she left her husband, there was a long and anxious year to get through before her daughter would have anything to do with her:

> "When I left my husband, I also left [my daughter], because he wouldn't leave. So in the end it was one of those terrible choices that you have to make. And she was very unhappy for a long time. She didn't like the woman I was having a relationship with either; she hated her, surprise, surprise. But she was only angry and upset and not having anything to do with me for about a year, and we have now got a really good, close relationship. I would say that I think I see more of her now than her dad does, and she is lovely; she is fine about it. I plucked up courage to tell her when she was about 14 or 15, which was like a nightmare! I sat down with her, and we were playing cards, and I said, I have got something to tell you. She just said, 'Yes, what?' and I said, I need to tell you that I am a lesbian. And she just looked at me and said, 'Yes, I know.' And I was like, what do you mean, you know? And she said, 'I have known for ages, how could I not have known?' So she was fine. That was a big relief then, that she was fine about it, and she is fine about my current partner and she gets on well with her. We have just taken it very slowly and she has been fine." (Elizabeth, 45)

For some children, the ideas they have in their own minds about what a lesbian is can be in stark contrast to what they know about their mother. For them, part of the task has to be to learn which story is the truth, what their mother tells them or what they hear in the playground. For others, the existing stereotypes can, unexpectedly, help them to make sense of what they are being told:

> "It's dificult at my age, really, to come out... Well, mainly it's been my sons. I didn't want them to find out second hand, and now I have come clean and told them. They accepted it; yes, I was surprised. I cried when I told my younger son. I said, I am sorry. And he said, 'Mum, I have known in one respect.' He said his mates had said to him,

> your Mum is a bit mannish, and he said, well, she brought us two boys up, she had to be male and female. He told me, 'Yes, I know, Mum, because you taught me football. I think I have learned more from you than I did from Dad.' So he wasn't entirely surprised." (Charis, 55)

However much we may want to protest that ideas about the 'mannish' lesbian are stereotypical and homophobic, the experience of Charis's son suggests that it may be important to talk them through carefully with children, rather than dismiss them out of hand.

Playground problems

Another powerful anxiety that lesbian mothers feel has to do with the real dilemma about how to protect and support their child against the homophobia of the world outside the family. It is one thing for an adult woman to come out and deal with the response, it is quite another to expect a young child to come out as having a gay mother. Unthinking homophobia is still an element in most children's social world. Although, as we have seen, there has been a massive shift in social attitudes towards homosexuality, this has not been reflected in most schools and playgrounds. Rather the opposite, in fact. Researchers generally report that homophobia is *more* commonly found in schools than in other social institutions, and words like 'gay', 'queer', or 'lezzie' are among the most frequently used insults in the playground. This is not down to the 'natural' behaviour of young children; rather it is a product of a particular social history.

In the United States the religious right have repeatedly stirred up moral panics about the threat posed to family life and the American way by gay schoolteachers. In a similar vein, the Conservative government of Margaret Thatcher tried to scare the electorate off voting for the opposition by claiming that Labour would teach vulnerable schoolchildren to be homosexual. At the 1987 Tory Party conference, Thatcher gave a chilling speech in which she warned that: "Children who need to be taught to respect traditional moral values are being taught that they have an inalienable right to be gay."[3] The notion that individuals do *not* have the right to be gay is profoundly alarming, but this approach led to the government of the time passing the notorious Section 28 (of the 1988 Local Government Act) which prohibits local authorities from funding "the promotion of homosexuality" or teaching in schools "the acceptability of homosexuality as a pretended family relationship". The impact of this poisonous piece of legislation on lesbian mothers should not be underestimated.

For an Act of Parliament to state that the relationship between a mother and her child is a "pretended family relationship" if that mother happens to be a lesbian is truly shocking. No other social group suffers legislative discrimination in this way. The impact on the children of lesbian parents is also immense. Despite the fact that this law does not and cannot apply to schools, teachers, governors and headteachers have often used the existence of Section 28 to justify their failure to address the issue. As I write this, the Labour government has still failed to meet its election promise to scrap the section (although one of the first acts of the Scottish Parliament was to abolish it), and the result has been to leave many schools, untouched by wider social shifts towards tolerance, as hotbeds of homophobia.

Lesbian mothers therefore fear, with good reason, that their children will be exposed to bullying and harassment at school and will get precious little support from teachers. Even when children are not actually being malicious, younger children can find it hard work and mothers may find they have to be more forthright, as Nicky explains: "I don't say the word 'lesbian'. I did once, to A's teacher. He wasn't getting harassed but the older kids were asking him questions, and he couldn't handle the attention. They were asking him too fast to handle; he is only seven."

For many mothers the fear of what their child may face at school is enough to convince them *not* to be honest and explicit with them:

> "It is difficult with the kids as well. We both have children. I have a 15-year-old, who I think would be quite cool about it, but she's going through a lot of

> problems of her own at the moment. I have a son of eleven who I think, in particular, would find it extremely difficult. There's so much negativity to being gay, and abuse of anyone related to being gay. There just seems to be so much homophobia at school." (Helen, 36)

As we have seen, older children may face more of a struggle coming to terms with their mother's sexuality anyway. On top of this, the transition to secondary school exposes them to a very different peer community and they face stronger pressures to conform than they will meet at any other time in their lives. The mothers who spoke to me all agreed that secondary school potentially represented a big headache. Ann and George, happily managing their blended family of six, were putting a lot of careful thought into how and when to tell their children as they prepared to set up home together:

A (37): At the time I wouldn't have said anything, because I was too busy bringing up three children. When you have one after another you don't stop and think about anything, really you don't.

G (41): Yes, I mean, the mother of three children puts herself last every time. You just do, don't you? We cannot be out. We have chosen not to be out here in Midchester; because it's not acceptable, you would get funny looks. And we have got six children who are not aware of what is going on, and it's not fair to them.

A: We are brewing up to that one!

G: We are going to tell them this summer, because we have lived as a couple, but separately, in separate households, for three years now, and it's not practical. And why should we? We are 40 years old, and we are living like teenagers, talking on the phone at midnight.

A: Every one of those six children is actually going to say, well, we know that, tell us something new!

G: We have decided what we are going to say to them. We are going to tell them that we are telling *them*, but we are not broadcasting it to the whole world. So, it's up to them. If they want to keep it to themselves, that's fine. But if they want to tell the whole world, that's fine too.

A: If they were all little children who were all under seven, if we had met then, then it would have been different. We would have moved in together and moved away and they would have grown up with it.

G: But we met each other with three teenagers each, virtually, and teenagers don't want to be different in any way; they have to be the same, don't they!

For Kaz, a disabled mother of three, it was important to find a way to arm her children with the right information before they moved up to secondary school. She was hopeful that the news wouldn't come as too much of a shock to them:

> "What about the kids? They don't know yet. I've got two at eleven and one at four, and they haven't got the faintest idea. I'm just trying to figure out a good time and place to tell them. I think, as far as the older ones are concerned, Mummy is Mummy no matter what. It's just finding the words to tell them, when they go to secondary school. I don't want to tell them three years down the line. I would like to tell them before they start secondary school, and they can get used to it.
>
> "We've got lesbians living not too far from us and [the kids] know, and it means nothing to them. I read *Diva* and stuff like that and leave it lying around the house, and they don't even ask." (Kaz, 34)

However strong the children are, however close their relationship with their lesbian mother, however accepting they may be, it seems inevitable that school will be a source of trouble rather than support.

It is profoundly unfair that these remarkable young people, many of whom seem to deal so astonishingly well with this big change in their lives, should have to put up with this. It is also unjust that their mothers, who already have more than enough to worry about, should have yet another source of anxiety:

> "[My kids] know the negative side as well. They know they can't go to school and say my mum's girlfriend this and that, because they might get hassle. That makes me feel horrible. My oldest one goes up to senior school next year and that worries me. So many kids are uneducated about things like that. I don't want them to have to go through that, but they will. But they are pretty strong and they are proud of me as well, so I think they will deal with it." (Charlotte, 30)

Despite the difficulties of family upheaval, and despite having to survive a school culture which seems far more likely to undermine than to support, lesbian mothers and their children do, on the whole, survive. Indeed, they do more than survive, they manage to achieve minor miracles against all the odds on a fairly regular basis. To come through such a storm, usually without outside support, with the mother/child relationship intact, is something to be proud of. And many of these women have very close relationships with their children.

> "I have two sons, and one of them I feel I can ask how his love life is going. I don't want all the details, but he can talk to me and I can talk to him about relationships in general, whether that is our current relationship or generally how we are in relationships, in the way that I might with a woman. But my other son, that's not happening at the moment." (Sue, 50)

Grandparents

Children don't just have parents, most of them have grandparents as well. And grandparents can be an enormously important influence on both children and their parents. What is more, some women are already grandmothers when they come out, and that can pose additional problems for *them*!

> "In my life, to come out openly would be destructive to a lot of people. I have got grandchildren, without bragging, who think I am the best thing since sliced bread, and for me to say, well, I am leaving Grandad and I am going to live with a woman would just so completely confuse them... I have this urge to go away from everybody and live on my own. Whether that's more to do with me, and mid-life crisis and helping other people all the time, or my sexuality, I'm not sure." (Barbara, 49)

Lesbian grandmother Barbara is trying to reconcile her sexuality with her deep sense of responsibility to her family. Many women told me that their own parents had tried just as hard to be supportive when their daughter came out to them, and this was obviously very helpful to their grandchildren. Sadly, however, some grandparents can cause serious problems for a lesbian mother. Grandparents who are deeply homophobic can cause great trouble, and may need to be firmly educated:

> "My son, from being very young, has mixed with all homosexual people, male, female, the whole lot, and I thought I was going to have a problem with him when he went up to senior school, and there has been no problem. Now he's of an age where he can understand what my relationship is with my present partner, and I also have two guys living with me who are also a couple, so he sees that as not unusual. Yet when my partner

> outed me to my mother, my mother immediately said she would go through legal channels to have my son removed from me, which was just like, bang! And then I thought, well, she can't do that. She's elderly, she's 78, so it was a shock, but she knows full well that she can't legally do anything. Her main concern was that he shouldn't be exposed to 'that sort of environment', but he's been exposed to it as a normal family unit. We all go out to work, we all go home, we sit and have a cup of coffee and we cook dinner: a very normal, boring life." (Jodie, 41)

This homophobic intervention from Jodie's elderly mother was very unhelpful and distressing, but at least there was no realistic possibility of her succeeding if she had followed through her threat of legal action. There was no angry father lurking in the background, and the courts were hardly likely to give Jodie's son into the care of an elderly woman (although grandparents have succeeded in getting custody in similar circumstances in the US). It can be very different when a child's father is involved:

> "When I left [my husband] Dan, my dad said if Dan wanted to get child custody of the boys he would support Dan. Two years after I left Dan the boys came to me and said, 'We don't want to go and stay with Dad again, we are too scared of him.' Dan's life was so stressed out... and he was therefore, quite logically but not rightly, taking it out on the boys. So I phoned him up and said, you are not having the boys this weekend. I will meet you, I will talk to you about it, get yourself a solicitor, I am going to court about this... And when I got home from this conversation with him, my father was on the phone saying, 'Right, I am coming up in two days' time, I am going to sort this out and I will give a lift to the boys so they can go to church with their dad.' And I said, hang on a second, you haven't asked why the boys don't want

> to go, it's not me... So I photocopied every piece of legal evidence that I had and sent it down to Dad with a letter. I gave it to Mum to give to him, but he never looked at it, and he wouldn't talk about it... He reads the *Daily Mail* or the *Telegraph* so I had to fight all that." (Nicky, 38)

This man's homophobia has, sadly, turned out to be a powerfully damaging and disruptive force in what was already a difficult situation for Nicky, her partner and her two sons.

Conclusion: happy families?

Of course, living as a lesbian with children is a challenge. Being a parent is far from easy, as anyone with kids will agree. In addition to all the usual problems and anxieties, lesbians have to deal with the effects of homophobia on their children's lives, and on their own relationships with them. The pain involved can be very deep, as can the feelings of guilt. Yet all the evidence is that children do adapt. They are, on the whole, remarkably resilient and inclined to be tolerant and accepting of the eccentricities of their mothers. The deep-rooted love that underpins the bonds between mothers and their children is precisely why family breakup can be so traumatic for all concerned. Yet it is also the reason why children want, very much, to be able to accept something that clearly makes their mum happy.

There can be no formula for success here. All children are individuals and every family has its own character and its own dynamic. But it does seem, from the evidence here, that children appreciate honesty and need to be given space and time to work out how to fit things into their lives. Mothers may have to grit their teeth and bear anger, rejection and upset from their children, particularly older ones. But, eventually, things seem to turn out remarkably well.

A lot depends on how self-confident the new lesbian mother is, and how at ease she feels about the transition she is asking her children to make. For some, this is a truly daunting experience. What makes it still more demanding is that lesbian mothers can be very isolated indeed.

Being a mum at home with young children is isolating enough for anyone, but when you find yourself the only lesbian mother for miles around, heterosexual normality can appear sadly tempting:

> "I think, if I had the option, it would be better to be the norm, for my kids. I haven't met any other lesbian mothers. I have found the whole thing really hard. I don't know if anybody who is gay with kids ever has a social life with their friends. I don't even know how you find that out." (Catherine, 40)

Mothers who feel guilt or anxiety about forcing their own life-choices on their children need to remember two things. Firstly, most of the problems faced by children of lesbian mums are less to do with relationship breakup than they are to do with the impact of social stigma. This is not your fault! With frank discussion, geared to their level of understanding, most kids can surmount the unpleasantness of homophobia. Secondly, there is evidence that a lesbian household is actually a very positive environment for children to grow up in.

For example, as Professor Diane Richardson stresses in her book *Women, Motherhood and Childrearing,* "The evidence is that children, especially girls, being brought up in a lesbian household are at far less risk of sexual abuse than children raised in a household with a male parent present."[4] She goes on to identify other benefits, including greater tolerance of diversity, and reminds us that, "There is no evidence to suggest that, as a group, children of lesbian mothers get picked on [at school] more than other children. Children are teased for all sorts of reasons."[5]

Of course, there can be such a thing as having children who are *too* well adjusted to the whole thing, as Michelle found out when she embarked on her first affair, with a woman older than her:

> "The trouble was, I went to her house and all her children still lived at home, and they were all older than I was. It was horrible. They were all just sat there, all had their children with them, and I just wanted to go home!

> ... At this time I was quite shy, and, of course, they were very open-minded, which I am now, but at the time I was a bit worried, to say the least! They all just waltzed into the bedroom, the oldest son with his two daughters. I was under the cover, with the cover up to my neck, not knowing what to do. [My lover] said, will you make us a cup of tea, and I said, no, I am not getting out of bed!" (Michelle, 30)

Fortunately, the shock of meeting her first girlfriend's alarmingly open-minded children didn't put her off; Michelle is now living happily as a lesbian and is very proud of her own daughter's open-mindedness!

Hearing these women speak about their efforts to do the best they could for their children, whilst not denying their own happiness, was very moving. Their achievements, in terms of creating new ways to live as a family, maintaining and strengthening their relationships with their children and refusing to give in to the homophobia of neighbours, schools and (all too often) their own parents, family and friends, were sometimes extraordinary. These adventurous families, working things out for themselves with no maps or guidebooks, are making a real and important contribution to social change. I have no doubt that the world will be a better place for all of us with them and their children in it. Queer communities everywhere should be very proud of their lesbian mums!

You don't expect to find a lesbian in a toddler group: May's story

May is a soft-spoken woman who works as a library assistant. When we spoke, over the phone, she had just turned 39 and was still thrilled to be discovering what it means to fall deeply in love for the first time. Her story of love arriving, out of the blue, in the middle of what seemed to be a run-of-the-mill married life, is as romantic as any novel.

However, this is no lesbian Mills & Boon. Between then, May and her partner have five children. May's oldest daughter was ten at the time of this interview. Although the tale of how two ordinary mums fell in love with each other on holiday, left their husbands and moved in together is a happy one, nothing can disguise the difficulties of coping with such a dramatic upheaval. This extraordinarily challenging transition is made more difficult when you don't happen to live in a big city with a major gay village and active lesbian support networks, and it doesn't help that the 'scene' still revolves around the needs of younger lesbians. Drinking, clubbing and pulling have little to offer two women who need to find out how on earth other lesbians manage to deal with two ex-husbands and five kids!

Reading May's story, it is hard not to be impressed by her determination and bravery. Without a trace of self-pity and with precious little support, she is setting about the task of creating a new kind of family that will not only be a safe and loving place for their five children, but will allow the wonderful new love she has found to flourish. She may not be alone – women all over the country are doing very similar things – but she is very isolated. And, when all is said and done, what *do* you tell the children?

*

I call myself a lesbian, though it isn't a word I would use with anyone who doesn't know me or anything. God, no! And it is not a word that has always described me. In the past, I don't know what word I would have used. I don't think I would have used anything! A few years ago, I wouldn't have labelled myself anything.

I was just growing up then. I am 39 now and I have only been a lesbian about two years. So, for most of my life, I would have just been an ordinary person. I didn't label myself with one thing or another, really.

Having said that, I don't really know now, particularly. Because I don't think the way I feel about myself has changed. Perhaps I am more straight than lesbian? I suppose, if you took somebody who knew right from their teenage years, I should think they are probably a different type of lesbian than I would be. I don't know. I am just looking at people we see. They seem to know where they are from day one! Whereas I think I am more heterosexually minded, in my style of life I mean, rather than in my sexual life, if that makes sense.

I don't know if it's easier for people these days, to come out. I suppose it *is* easier. There are more things to do, but I never gave it a thought when I was young, apart from one panicky moment! Then I thought, oh, no, that can't be me and then forgot about it. I can't believe that one thing made me scared about it for the rest of my life; that's not what I'm saying, but it only occurred to me very recently.

That panicky moment was a schoolteacher crush, and I thought, no, that's not me! I put it in the back of my mind, enough to last all this time! Lots of young girls have crushes and you just put it down to your age.

Well, then, two years ago I went on holiday with a friend; she's the mother of two children. My friend's elder daughter and the middle one of my three daughters had been best friends at school and, like you do, we went to 'toddlers' together and were friends together. So we went away for a week, took the children away for a holiday, and we just fell in love.

We were two ordinary women, with husbands, and we fell in love with each other, and we are together now, with five children. It was extraordinary. Neither of us was particularly happy in our marriages anyway. I think, if you are happy, you don't look for other things. But we have always been close, close friends. I think, being together all the time and being away, it was very gradual. I felt it a little bit, and then I wasn't sure if I was getting feedback!

Obviously, being both ordinary women as we were, it's very difficult! You think, "Well, hang on, I'm not sure if I am right or not," and you can't make a mistake because you might lose a friend. So it was very slow and gradual. But it just got to a point where we both realised, and it became an overwhelming thing that changed our lives.

Before that, something occurred to me about two or three years ago. It was something my mum said to me. Because I had been married twice, and she said, "You always pick the wrong men." I followed it through to its logical conclusion and thought, well, *why* do I pick the wrong men? Then I thought, perhaps it's because they are men! I just thought it through. Before that, I had always had women on my 'list', pop stars, you know. Then, when I started thinking along those lines everything else started to make sense. The way I feel about myself and who I am as a person, and it all started falling into place.

So then I said, to a long-term friend who I was at school with since we were eleven, "I think I like women." And she said, "Perhaps you do, perhaps you don't. If you do, you are not the stereotypical type." We don't believe in stereotypes, so she said, if I was gay she wouldn't be surprised. So I made a decision that, well, OK, I will be with my children until they are old enough to look after themselves and then I will find out for myself.

I had sort of made that decision, but I didn't expect to find anybody at this time in my life because I was going to look after my children first. So it was a total surprise, a real bolt from the blue. It was very scary, actually, at the time.

Because I did fall in love with my two husbands, I fancied them. At least, I thought I did. Obviously, because you wouldn't go do far down the road of marriage if you didn't think you were in love. But now, having experienced this relationship with a woman, they *were* attractive and I cared for them, but I don't think I really loved them wholeheartedly. After all, I've left both of them.

The first one I married too young, anyway. I was just 20, and that's miles too young. I did love him at first, but then it just didn't go anywhere. It wasn't what I wanted, it wasn't right. So I left. With the second, it was harder to leave because I had the children this time, whereas before I didn't have any. I was working and financially viable, and then you can just go. But if you are dependent on the husband for money, it is harder to leave. Also, if you've got children, you don't want to deprive them of their father. So I would have stayed. I wouldn't have been happy for the rest of our married life. We had not been happy for the last five out of the ten years we were together, I would say, but I wouldn't have chucked it in for nothing, just to leave the kids struggling on their own without anybody. It was only them that made me stay. But, once she and I found each other, well, we couldn't stay after that. You can't stay with the wrong person once you've found the right person.

When I told my husband he wasn't surprised about me leaving really; he didn't show any real shock. But he *was* shocked when I told him who I was leaving *with*. He couldn't believe that. He was in a bit of a state then; that did surprise him! But sex was never good between us; I put up with it, more than actually wanting it. So he didn't seem to be totally shocked and stunned.

With sex, I think the trouble is that you just try and follow what you're told. I suppose, unless it's really obvious [that you're a lesbian] right from when you are young, you just follow the set patterns. You follow the norm, don't you, the norm that is portrayed to you. You don't think of anything outside of it. I obviously didn't have very strong feelings [for women] when I was young, or not strong enough to come through. Obviously now sex is totally different, but then I never actually enjoyed it at all; I never expected to really. I just thought there was something wrong with me, that I was frigid or prudish or whatever the words are. I thought there was something wrong with me and my body, not that I was with the wrong sex! When I was with my girlfriend it was a new experience, and still is.

I regret lost years. I wish I had known a long time ago. I am getting old and past it now, and I've not started yet! Everything is better, it's a much better relationship than any I've ever experienced. We have communication, we think alike, we speak in the same way. I read that book, *Men are from Mars, Women are from Venus* [by John Gray], and there was a bit in there that said you have to interpret what men say and make sense of it. I thought, why should we? It's much nicer talking to someone who knows where you are coming from! We have the same logic pattern! If we fall out, which we don't very often, we communicate sensibly and we get back together. It's just the closeness. There's no power struggle either, there is no power game going on. We are just equal, and we poodle along on a level together. It really is lovely.

I think, in hindsight, it is difficult to make a judgement that's not clouded, but if I look back on the person that I was, I think, how could I have been so stupid! I must have been a slow learner, but I can't believe I lasted 38 years before I realised! But I don't know how it could have happened sooner, because we fell in love, and that just happens. If someone had said to me, you are going to be falling in love with this woman who you know and you have known since you were at 'toddlers' together, I would never have believed it in a million years, because you don't expect to find a lesbian in a toddler group, and nor did she.

But the pressure to follow convention is so strong. Nobody would choose to be on the outside of what's acceptable really; you wouldn't choose prejudice and stigma for yourself, would you, so you don't consider it as a possibility. We have lost friends. We are quite content with each other's company, but a lot of people have added two and two and made five, and we have had a lot of people ignoring us. We haven't moved. I am in my original house, and we all moved in together; it is big enough, just. So we are still in the area where people all knew us before, and we have had a lot of cold-shoulder treatment. We are 'out' in the sense that everybody knows we are here, but we are not 'out' out. We haven't actually openly declared that we are together because of the children. We are concerned about them, we don't want them to get any stick at school. It would be much easier to say, well, yes, we are together, so bugger off. But it's the kids really; we are trying to make their life as smooth as possible, so we have said that we are just sharing the house because we can't afford not to, which is fairly plausible.

We are all right for moral support because our families have been very good. We have been very lucky that our families have all taken it very well. We have lost a lot of friends, but they are not true friends. Nobody has got the guts to actually say anything to us, they just ignore us and look at us as if we're a bit weird. These are people who knew us before and were quite happy to talk to us. Our true friends are still with us, but those kind of people we just ignore picking the kids up from school, instead of chatting to and passing the time of day with.

The kids are all right. So far they are all quite young; the oldest one is ten, and they have all accepted it without really questioning it. They occasionally make the odd joke and they do a little nursery rhyme about us kissing up in a tree. But then, they joke about us being 'lezzies' and next thing they go on about us getting boyfriends. We haven't actually said anything. They know we are happy and they know we are affectionate and warm to each other, but at the moment they are still too young to have their innocence removed. So we are on our own, because we don't know, if we get problems in the future, how to deal with them.

My middle daughter has got a little boy at school calling her 'queer' and 'bent' and one of his parents has put two and two together. She is having trouble with him. At the moment we are ignoring it, because he is just a silly little boy; he has just learnt a new word and is flashing it about. But when we get problems with our children, homophobic problems, we don't know what we will do. I assume we will get more problems when they are teenagers and want to bring their friends round. I am dreading it, really, but we are alone in that respect. We are isolated, because we don't know anybody else in our situation. We have survived together a year without too much trouble. I imagine it getting worse as they get older, but I suppose they will just have to choose their friends carefully!

The children are definitely OK. They are not suffering. Considering their family has split up, they haven't had any problems in school or been traumatised or anything. They are a lot happier. My eldest daughter is a lot happier than she was, because my husband was a very negative person and she used to worry a lot and take it all on board; she is a little worrier. But she has come out of herself so much this year, with all the pressure taken off and the relaxed atmosphere at home. She is a different girl.

Also, there being two of us helps, because we are still a family unit. If you are on your own as a single parent you have got the whole worry of everything by yourself. Because there are two of us, any of our adult worries we share between ourselves and don't pass down to the children. I think that helps, that there are two adults in the house and they can see that everything is smoother and happier and generally for the best.

There is no way I would go back to men! Even if this all fell through, which I don't think it will, because we are too suited, there is no way I would ever go back to men. They are just not right for me. At first I thought I had changed. Then I thought, I don't know if I have changed, I think I have just realised something! But that's depressing. I can't believe it's taken me so long. But it's wonderful now.

Notes

1. The 'science' behind such research is dubious. Interested readers are referred to Edward Stein's scholarly book, *The Mismeasure of Desire: The science, theory and ethics of sexual orientation*, Oxford University Press, Oxford, 1999, for a critical overview of the field. His account of the scientist who took his students for a boat trip to look for lesbian seagulls is very funny.
2. For up-to-date information and advice, contact Stonewall (details in the resources section at the end of the book).
3. For an account of this speech and its impact, see Tamsin Wilton, *Antibody Politic: AIDS and society*, New Clarion Press, Cheltenham, 1991.
4. Diane Richardson, *Women, Motherhood and Childrearing*, Macmillan, London, 1993.
5. Ibid.

4

NEW ME, NEW LIFE?

"It was a mixture of frightening and exciting at the same time. I actually thought, when it was happening to me, how could I ever be normal again? My life can never be the same again. I saw it as a really black future; that I can't be me any more. Of course I can, but at that time I found it really frightening. But the feelings I was experiencing, I found really exciting as well." (Paula, 40)

As we saw in the previous chapter, coming out as a lesbian is particularly challenging for women who have to support their children through the transition. There are, however, other challenges to be faced by the 'new' lesbian, who may feel rather like a child herself as she tries to settle into an unfamiliar life. There are new pleasures to be enjoyed, new ways of being to explore and many new relationships to be nurtured or established. Newly out women have many kinds of 'lesbian' relationships to adjust to and they may have to work out different ways of being themselves in existing relationships as well.

How does this major life-change impact on long-standing relationships with parents, workmates and friends? What about breaking the news to boyfriends or husbands? And how do women manage to adjust to the unfamiliar prejudices of the wider community, or to explore the new community they suddenly find themselves a member of?

Here it becomes increasingly hard to find points of commonality in women's stories. After all, each of us comes to lesbian life with a unique collection of relationships and at a different stage in her life. You will therefore find fewer clearly identified themes in this chapter. Rather than impose an artificial thematic structure, I have drawn on the idea that each one of us lives at the centre of an onion of relationships. The inner layers encompass those closest to us – parents, lovers and children – and the outer layers represent those we feel more distant from, including, at the outermost layers, abstract ideas like 'society'.

The key question asked here is, what is the difference between heterosexual life and lesbian life at each layer of the onion? From the perspective of these women, who have experienced both, the answer seems to be that almost everything is different. At every level of our lives, from the one-to-one of close relationships to the more abstract question of how we fit in as members of society, changing sexual identity has an impact. But let's start with that mysterious space at the heart of the onion, and explore how women's sense of themselves and who *they* are changes as they come out.

The real me?

Perhaps not surprisingly, women tended to feel that they had become more confident and assertive as a result of leaving heterosexuality behind:

> "I think that one of the things that has happened to me, definitely, is that I have got more confident over the last few years. Because I have developed personally, if you like, so I'm not as submissive; I'm not as easily controlled, which I used to be." (Paula, 40)

It is not difficult to imagine why this might be so. The process of recognising prohibited sexual feelings, deciding to act on those feelings and/or to change your identity accordingly is a challenge.

Whatever the circumstances, any woman who embarks on such a bold venture has to draw on reserves she may not have realised she had. There is nothing like surviving a crisis to make you recognise strengths you never knew you possessed.

Perhaps more significantly, the traditional power dynamics of heterosexuality keep women in second place. Women in relationships with men are still expected to behave with self-sacrifice and, yes, submission. Whilst individual women may not be submissive to individual men, the business of managing a marriage and bringing up children requires them to sacrifice their own needs for the greater good of the family unit. It is difficult for heterosexual couples to break away from this ancient script, however much they may want to and however hard they try. Men are simply taken more seriously than women are, they have greater social status and both sexes are socialised into taking this pretty much for granted.

Virginia spoke very powerfully about the shift in self-esteem she experienced when she became a lesbian:

> "What I have gained from my relationship with women is being a different kind of woman, and to be a woman I can be proud of. I don't think I could be proud of the woman I was when I was heterosexual." (Virginia, 44)

Escaping from this dynamic can feel very powerful, as any recently divorced woman can confirm. When you add to this new sense of freedom the experience – exceedingly rare in the lives of most women – of being in a relationship with someone very skilled in giving love and support, the sense of power and resilience can be very heady indeed. This kind of independence is extremely hard to come by in relationships with men:

> "I like the feeling of autonomy and power it gives me; not power over somebody else, but power over myself, I guess. The independence, the freedom to be more as I want: the rules don't apply to me." (Robbie, 48)

Another phenomenon which some women commented on is that, ironically, once the pressure to relate to men as a potential sexual partner has been removed, it becomes much easier to relax and enjoy their company. Sometimes, as in Zara's case, this is particularly so with gay men:

> "One of the strange things is that I love being with gay men... I identified a couple of men in Meetings [Quaker worship] who I thought were gay, and I thought, at least I am not on my own. Then I went to the first national conference I have been to with church and the most amazing thing I got out of that conference was that I could relax with men, because there was no other agenda." (Zara, 39)

Interestingly, questions of appearance, of weight, physical attractiveness and beauty were almost entirely absent from these interviews. It took me a while to realise just how significant this absence is. We are, after all, constantly told we live in a society which is obsessed with the way women look. Everywhere, women of all ages are putting themselves through physical tortures of various kinds – diets, compulsive exercise, cosmetic surgery – in order to be sexually attractive to men. Femininity in contemporary industrialised nations *means* to be consumed with doubt about our looks. So it is quite extraordinary that such a long series of interviews, in which women were encouraged to reflect upon their sexual and emotional lives and relationships and to consider their history as sexual beings, contain almost no mention of looks. Katie, however, did find herself becoming concerned about her appearance:

> "Initially I found it a lot harder to go to bed with a woman because we were the same, only I have always been a little bit on the large side! So it was, am I bigger than her? Have I got bigger hips? And so that was a problem in the very early stages, because I had the same female body but I had a bit more cellulite. So that made

> it a bit harder, but once I got over that it was a lot easier." (Katie, 26)

The fact that her discomfort stands out as unusual in these accounts suggests that the escape from heterosexuality is often an escape from the remorseless cultural pressure on women to judge our own attractiveness constantly. This, in itself, may be empowering and may contribute to a greater sense of self-esteem for many women.

Sapphic bliss

The most obvious difference between living a heterosexual life and living as a lesbian is the quality of intimate sexual relationship. Predictably, when I asked women to pinpoint the difference between the new life and the old, it was the wonders of lesbian love itself that most readily sprang to their lips:

> "Oh, yes! It was like, whatever I had been doing beforehand [with men], why had I wasted twenty years doing that? It's not in the same league. Sex is not a nice word; it's making love, and what I was doing beforehand wasn't making love, but this is... It's just lighting up a fuse. Yes, if you've never had chocolate cake you can't miss it, but once you've had it you are not going to go back to bread and butter." (Ann, 37)

As we have already seen in an earlier chapter, women found sex dramatically more pleasurable with female partners than they ever had with men. But there is more to a good relationship than sex, and there seem to be other reasons why women found other women to be better at relationships than men. For Katie who, at 26, was young enough to be familiar with non-traditional 'new' men, the key difference was still emotional. Although she admitted to a simple aesthetic preference for women's bodies, she stressed that women's emotional openness made it easier to trust them:

> "[Women] are more aesthetically pleasing. I trust them more. I think women get more emotionally involved, whereas men are very physically based. I wouldn't trust them for two seconds; I think they would run off with anything presented to them. You just get more emotional involvement with a woman." (Katie, 26)

For others, being in a relationship with a woman seemed to make it possible for them to fall deeply in love for the first time. When in relationships with men, Fiona had been cynical about such romantic notions:

> "I would have been sceptical about love at first sight, and I would have said I think love breaks down into just affection and familiarity. But it's really different when you are properly in love with somebody. I think probably not a day goes by when you don't look at them and remember those feelings. And that's not affection, and that's not just from being familar." (Fiona, 35)

Of course, you could say that this was just a case of not having met the right person, of whatever sex. But what seems to lie at the heart of the new intensity of romantic feelings, which was expressed by many of these women, is something to do with trust, safety and intimacy. As Fiona puts it, "Well, my immediate thought was that there was an incredible freshness which was rewarding personally in a very surprising way, and the extent of the relationship really was so much deeper than I had known with anyone else."

This experience, of an intimacy that was somehow *deeper* than anything possible with a man, was described over and over again. For some, the most significant aspect of it all was simple. "It's the tenderness, I suppose, and the emotion," said Maureen, 34, "something that you just don't get with a man."

The ability of their female lovers to offer this tenderness and emotional openness was a new experience for women who had been trying to find these things with men, and was something that they clearly found to be both exciting and emotionally nourishing:

> "I find that men are just so different and I find women are more interesting. This is a huge generalisation because obviously there are some interesting men out there, but I find women more open in the main. I find that the kind of thought processes that women go through are just more in-depth and more stimulating. Basically, I enjoy women's company a lot more... If I had found men to offer the emotional, enriching and nourishing stuff too, then perhaps I could have gone down that road... because it's not an unpleasant experience, or it hasn't been for me." (Kate, 26)

These women, having spent varying amounts of time participating in intimate sexual relationships with men, are uniquely well placed to offer insights into the emotional skills of women and men. And what they generally expressed was the feeling that something is simply *absent* in emotional relationships with men. Fifty-year-old Jodie had no doubt what the difference was: "What's missing with a man? It is an intimacy that's missing, I think. And you know that intimacy there is between two women, and the way you say a word, or there's a gesture or a look or whatever?"

There was remarkably little bitterness in these accounts. Very few of the women were dismissive about men or hostile towards them, so these are not the rantings of man-haters. On the contrary, when they tried to pinpoint the differences between the sexes as partners in intimate relationships, most were very careful *not* to slag off men in general or their former partners in particular. I got the impression that these were issues they had given some thought to. So it is interesting that so many seemed to reach similar conclusions; namely that the emotional closeness we all look for in our love relationships is made much easier when the partners are equal:

> "They are a lot more equal, relationships with women. I think there isn't the power thing, and in the sexual relationship as well, there isn't the power thing really; there is a lot more [that is] equal." (April, 45)

Although the difficulties women have in their intimate relationships with men are fairly well recognised in wider society, women are made to feel responsible for overcoming men's emotional backwardness. In short, women have to work hard at making sense of men, in order that heterosexual relationships can function. Women who leave men to live a lesbian life don't see why they should do this. Why should they work so hard, and with so little reward, when there is an alternative available? Such women are in no doubt about the benefits of lesbian relationships. Remember May's enthusiastic words:

> "Everything! It's a much better relationship, we have communication, we think alike, we speak in the same way. I read that book, *Men are from Mars, Women are from Venus* [by John Gray], and there was a bit in there that said you have to interpret what men say and make sense of it, and I thought, why should we really? It's much nicer talking to someone who knows where you are coming from! There is not a power struggle either, we are just equal and we just poodle along on a level together, it really is lovely." (May, 39)

This is, perhaps, one of the unintended consequences of the way in which heterosexual relationships have been organised. If men are socialised into being detached from their emotions, poor at intimacy and unable to communicate, women have had to become super-skilled at these things, in order to have any chance of relating to men. This means that the emotional intimacy and communication between two women can be extraordinary:

> "I think the closeness, being on the same wavelength with feelings, just everything... The knowing that we

> know what we like and things like that, just being on the same wavelength as another woman." (Jodie, 41)

Women of a younger generation were just as likely as their older sisters to find men hopelessly unskilled at intimacy. If things are changing (and, as the mother of a son I hope and think that they are), they are doing so very slowly. Kate, one of the younger women who took part, thought that external inequalities between women and men had a very negative impact on heterosexual relationships, and enjoyed the freedom from such expectations in lesbian relationships:

> "I feel that you are on a level; there is no dictated-by-society expectation of your behaviour; you are both coming from the same place." (Kate, 26)

Whatever the reasons, lesbian partners are clearly able to offer something quite new to women accustomed to the emotional incompetence of men. In many cases, this came as a wonderful relief, and the language women used to describe this new-found contentment is very telling. They spoke of comfort, safety, warmth, being on the same wavelength, nourishment, richness, being at ease. Several described it as being like 'coming home'. As one put it:

> "With a woman I am more comfortable. Things with women are more caring; they know what I want and I know what they want, but I can't point to one thing. Being on the same wavelength, knowing each other, more comfortable." (Michelle, 30)

The downside

Of course, lesbian relationships have their share of difficulties too, and it can be devastating to find that out just as you have convinced yourself that they are the nearest thing to heaven on earth. Lesbian relationships may lack some of the common problems that dog heterosexuality, but they can be beset with difficulties of their own. Indeed, the very strengths of lesbian relationships can also have a difficult side. For example, clearer communication makes it less easy to just let things slide:

> "I would say relationships with women are much more difficult, because women are more upfront about saying, I am not happy about this and it should change, or, I think we should do this. They are much more willing to talk about things when they are going wrong or when they are going right, but more open, so you have to work harder at it, and I don't think women let you get away with things like men do... If you both get PMT at the same time, the windows blow out, whereas it's not the same with a man, because they just write it off, tread round you carefully. Whereas another woman will say, what the hell's the matter with you and why am I getting the end of this, it's not fair." (Elizabeth, 45)

While Elizabeth was acknowledging that she found this difficult, from what she said there is an important distinction to be made between *difficult* and *bad*. All relationships are difficult and require hard work. It is likely to be the case that bringing things out into the open and confronting them makes for a better relationship in the end, however unpleasant the process may be. However, there are other potential problems specific to lesbian relationships that are more straightforwardly negative.

These problems generally spring from the fact that we live in a homophobic environment. This means that lesbian relationships are lived out in greater isolation than most heterosexuals can imagine. The social institutions that exist to help prop up families – schools, relationship guidance, social services, religious organisations, family doctors – are geared to heterosexuality. What is more, fear of homophobia means that most lesbian relationships must be kept secret from at least somebody. This may mean 'de-dyking' the flat when parents visit, cooking up a plausible story for the landlord, being very careful what you say to teachers at parents' evenings, not kissing your lover goodbye in full sight of the neighbours or not holding hands in the street. It can be especially difficult at those times when heterosexuals feel most relaxed – on holidays abroad, for example, or at the local multiplex cinema with the kids.

Living with these external stresses can feel a bit like trying to have a relationship in a pressure cooker. It is not surprising that many relationships cannot take such strains:

> "The turnover with gay relationships is really high, so I just don't know if it's going to work... I know so many more people who are straight who are in relatively sane, steady, long-term relationships than I know people who are gay. They all seem to be going through so much crap." (Kerry, 32)

If you come to lesbian relationships with high expectations and, let's be honest, many of us do for one reason or another, then a series of disappointments can leave you feeling very angry and disillusioned. This was clearly the case for Karla who, at 26, had not yet managed to sustain a relationship with a woman, "A couple of years ago I could have said I liked women because I am sexually attracted [to them] and they are good company and they treat me right. But no, women don't, all the women that I have had relationships with have all been complete cows."

Another pressure on lesbian couples comes from the lesbian community itself. Again, it is understandable that we all want to present a rosy picture of lesbianism to the outside world. After all, the heterosexual majority is quite happy to hold us up to scorn and derision, and to tell us that our relationships are immature, perverted, disgusting and doomed to failure. So, of course we have to cling on to our belief that we have something unique and precious. As, indeed, we do. But the need to justify ourselves constantly can mean that we deny or conceal problems and lay too much stress on the good things:

> "At least the inequalities between men and women we all know about; they are all spoken about, even if men don't want to recognise them... I think they are very hidden in lesbian relationships because there is the sense that, well, they must be more equal between two women." (Eve, 42)

It is, sadly, not possible for individual women to eradicate the complex impact of homophobia on their relationships. But the good news is that the network of support for lesbian and gay couples is growing. Helplines and specialist support groups are to be found in many regions and existing organisations – including Relate and social services – are starting to recognise their responsibilities to people who don't conform to the narrow heterosexual norm. Hopefully, such developments point to a time when our relationships will not have to be lived in a pressure cooker of secrecy.

My wife left me for another woman

In the next layer of the onion are those people we might expect to cause plenty of difficulty for the new lesbian: her male partner and her parents. For most men, it will be extremely difficult to come to terms with the fact that their wife is now a lesbian. Along with all the feelings of loss and rejection associated with the end of a relationship, they also have to deal with the fact that their entire sex has been found wanting. Since heterosexual prowess is still regarded as one of the tests of a 'real' man, being told that you don't measure up to a woman must be upsetting on many levels.

Of course, some women did have stories to tell about manipulative or abusive husbands. Yet, perhaps surprisingly, such stories were very much in the minority. When they spoke about their husbands at all, most women were at pains to stress that they were decent, well-meaning people who could not be held responsible for their move towards lesbianism. Many would agree with Liz (42), who stressed, "It's no fault of my husband's. This is what was really hard for me to do, to leave that marriage, because he was so good and understanding."

Far from being selfish bastards, some husbands seem to have been remarkably supportive of their lesbian wives. Again, Liz was not unusual in reporting that her husband had been able to respond to her change in sexuality very positively: "But even he said, this is the best thing you could have done for both of us."

There may be reasons why some men are able to accept the news that their wife is a lesbian with a degree of equanimity. In some senses it lets them, and the marriage, off the hook if their wife had been a lesbian all along. After all, a man can hardly be expected to succeed as the sexual partner of a woman who is 'naturally' attracted to women, and this can offer a get-out clause from rejection and injured pride.

Of course, some men handle the situation very badly. Nevertheless, it is reassuring to know that, in the right circumstances, ending the marriage can be a journey both partners take together:

> "I persuaded [my husband] to come into counselling with me... At the end of four months we felt we were going to end our relationship and deal with the children and family... We both managed to journey together, both of us were doing moving at the same time, which made it much easier and it meant that there wasn't any anger, as it never emerged. We were both letting each other go at the same time." (Zara, 39)

Sometimes the bonds between husband and wife feel so strong that the two of them agree to try and maintain the marriage and make space within it for the wife to have affairs with women lovers:

> "Well, we have an exceptionally close relationship... We have always been able to talk about anything. He is very supportive and he said, basically, look, if you are gay you are gay, and you can't sit around being celibate all your life, because it's changed. And it's one of those things that we are going to have to put up with." (Louise, 32)

People of all genders and sexual preferences may opt for such 'open' relationships, and many a life-long marriage has been kept alive by allowing one or both partners the freedom to take lovers. The pitfalls – jealousy, the risk of unexpectedly falling in love, unequal numbers of lovers, one partner being more committed to the idea than the other – are well known, and must be anticipated in marriages which try to make space for a lesbian wife. I suspect, too, that the differences between men and women, which have emerged in this research as so significant, would become very hard to manage under such circumstances. Theresa and her husband considered this as a possibility, but eventually rejected it:

> "We looked at the possibility of staying within the marriage and having partners, but we worked out that in the long term it wouldn't work for us... In fact, he was more supportive than anybody; even the only gay woman I knew gave me no support at all." (Theresa, 49)

It is reassuring to learn that men are capable of being so supportive of women who leave them to set off as lesbians. However, I do want to add a note of caution. We have heard a lot about men's lack of sensitivity, and the ones who offer such extraordinary levels of support are the exception rather than the rule. Most women had chosen not to tell their husbands about their new sexual choices, particularly when there were children involved. It is not possible to know what these men's reactions might be, but the very fact that they were *not* told suggests that those who knew them had reason to anticipate a hostile response.

Other women described a scenario where a marriage had clearly deteriorated long before their own sexuality became an issue. In these circumstances, it is just one of a number of factors in their husband's behaviour towards them:

> "So I told him, and I stayed for another year because he was taking a college course. I made the bargain (in my head, not telling him) that I would stay with him until

> he finished his course. But he was making such a mess of the course, blaming me for so much stuff, and not putting any effort into keeping our relationship going, that I thought, bugger him, I am going!" (Nicky, 38)

If husbands and male partners can help or hinder a woman who is trying to establish herself in her new lesbian identity, so too can parents. Where both parents are still living, mothers and fathers may react quite differently to the news, and may end up playing quite distinct roles in relation to their 'new' daughter:

> "Having an Indian dad, and my mum's an English Catholic and very naive... When I told her a few months ago she said, are you sure you just haven't met the right man? And I said, no, I just haven't met the right woman. And she thought of me as having a friend; she just couldn't see that it was a proper partner, she couldn't get it. [My dad] was completely fine. I thought he wouldn't speak to me again, but he said that I mustn't lie to myself and he was really angry that I had hidden it for so long. I got my brother to tell him, because I couldn't bear to, and he phoned me straight away and said, I love you and it's fine." (Claire, 39)

There is no clear pattern in the responses of parents. It is not the case that fathers always find it easier than mothers, or vice versa. Michelle's parents, for example, reacted in the opposite way to Claire's: "He [my dad] likes my partner, but he doesn't really accept it now. But my mother is fine, it is like having a second daughter to her."

In fact, the response of parents seems to be fairly unpredictable. Some surprise their daughters by being calm, accepting and supportive, whilst others behave really quite badly. I suspect most readers will be horrified at the behaviour of these parents:

> "My mum... was screaming and shouting and said, 'You are going to get really, really hurt,' and all this kind of

> bullshit came out. And then my stepdad came in, and then every time any of my friends came into the house he used to say things like, 'Oh, have you got a carrot in your bag, love?' and stuff like that." (Karla, 26)

On the other hand, most of us would be happy to get the kind of support this woman got from her father:

> "Dad… tried to help out as best he could, and when I met the woman I live with now he was great about that too. He's dead now, but insofar as he funded our first house he was really giving us his blessing." (Hilary, 40)

Coming out to one's parents is famously hard to do, and even the most in-your-face dyke may be firmly in the closet around her mum and dad. So it is no surprise that many women confirmed that their parents have yet to be told. Kerry who, in her 30s, found herself living with her parents for a while, maintains a 'neither in nor out' situation, which is probably familiar to many:

> "I am not out to my parents but the door is wide open and should they want to step in it won't be very difficult for them. I make it as easy as possible without actually saying anything, because for good Irish mothers, if they don't talk about it, then it's not a problem." (Kerry, 34)

New kid on the block: the support of the lesbian community

There can be no doubt that the existence of a visible lesbian community is important to most lesbians. Indeed, it would not be possible to lead a lesbian life without it. You can argue that there is no such thing as *the* lesbian community, rather there are many local lesbian communit*ies* in different regions. It would also be true to say that the realities of discrimination *within* the lesbian world mean that some marginalised groups of women – Black lesbians, those who are disabled, older lesbians and others – have established their own subcommunities. However, I would argue that there is, indeed, such a thing as *the* lesbian community. By this I mean the overarching subculture that includes everything from specialist lesbian publications such as *Diva* to support networks, social groups, bars and clubs. Heterosexuals are generally blithely unaware of the existence of this community (I speak from experience!), and yet its norms help define what it means to be a lesbian today.

Many women who adopt a lesbian identity later in their lives have an existing circle of friends. If they feel secure enough in these friendships to come out, and if the response is supportive, they are less likely to need the support of local lesbians:

> "The support of heterosexual friends has been really important too. When they have said, yes, I can acknowledge why you would feel like that, and they don't necessarily have to feel it themselves... In some ways they have been just as, if not more, important [than the lesbian community] because they are an established group of friends that I had and still have. And I'm not separatist in my lifestyle at all; a lot of my friends do happen to be gay/lesbian/bisexual, but a lot of them are also heterosexual. My friends have been fantastic. Yes, I am lucky!" (Kate, 26)

At 26, Kate's friends are likely to be young people with relatively tolerant attitudes. For older women struggling to leave the heterosexual mainstream for lesbian life, the community and its activities offer a vital lifeline. Many women mentioned *Diva* and the social group Kenric and said how useful they had been. Some had met partners through contact ads in the gay press:

> "It was really isolating, because I didn't know any other gay people. I felt so isolated. What I did in the end was I actually put an advert in the *Pink Paper* and I met quite a

> few women… I met a couple and we became really good friends and I used to go out with them, and that's how I got on to the scene and that's how I met my partner, that was the only way I could get to meet people." (Liz, 42)

> "I started to read lesbian literature; I started reading *Diva* and anything I could get my hands on. Then, of course, one thing leads to another and you start looking out for women who are lesbians; tennis clubs are rife with them, and I met my first girlfriend there, and she's still a friend now." (Claire, 39)

Women who live unthinkingly in the heterosexual mainstream may find it difficult to understand why the 'virtual' lesbian community of websites, books and magazines is so important. Perhaps if they stopped to think, they might recognise the extent to which their own sense of security in their female role is bolstered by women's glossies, fashion pages and certain TV programmes! For lesbians, these resources are often the only time we see our image reflected back to us accurately. For at least one woman, the services on offer through this virtual community enabled her to explore her sexuality before taking the plunge and coming out:

> "I was getting a bit desperate at home because I thought, what if I leave home and then suddenly get into a relationship with a woman and think, oh no, this is not what I want at all? I am going to have to have sex with somebody to make sure that this is what I want. So I had to pay for it in the end, but it did the trick, because at least then I knew that it was the kind of sex that I wanted. [It was] madness, I think, complete madness. I was lucky, because my husband took my daughter away on holiday, and so I had a week on my own and I rang up this number, I found it in *Diva*, and this girl came over. She came over twice actually, I just wanted to make sure!" (April, 45)

For lesbians who are old hands at the 'scene' and who take it for granted, the enthusiastic reaction of newcomers can be a salutory reminder of its importance:

> "In Asia there are no lesbian groups; you don't have any gay bars, so I didn't even know there was any literature on the subject until I got back to England two years go. I was completely gobsmacked, I went round absorbing everything like a teenager." (Kerry, 34)

Yet the lesbian 'scene' can sometimes seem a feeble creature indeed once you venture out of the centre of London or Manchester. For those women who have not yet managed to track it down, there can be a real sense of isolation:

> "At the moment we have no contact with [local lesbian groups] because we have had trouble finding anything. We are in the middle of Surrey and there doesn't seem to be anything around. We phoned a helpline a few times just to try and find organisations. We have heard of Kenric, but I don't seem to be able to track that down either, so we are just on our own." (May, 39)

The gay 'scene' of clubs, pubs and social events is of very real importance in lesbian life. This should not be underestimated. However, nor is it without its problems. For many women, coming to terms with the limitations of the scene is part and parcel of the process of coming out. Problem number one: it is dominated by (wealthier, more confident) men, as many women have discovered.

> "So I found the gay scene myself by looking through the magazines... But that was a long process because I went to mixed clubs to find they were all male-dominated, it was like, where were the lesbians?" (Theresa, 35)

Problem number two: as well as being full of men, it is very young!

> "I rang the Lesbian Line and they were fine, really nice. I met two girls at this coffee house place, and they invited me out on the scene, but I have always had a problem with that, with going out on the scene. It just seems very young generally, and I'm not... So the scene is not something that I have really fallen into comfortably... I do go out sometimes on the scene in Leeds. Women seem to be getting less and less [in number], and men seem to be getting more and more... And the gay women who do go are younger; it's just a younger element.
>
> "This is my mission; where are they? I think they have got to be out there somewhere!" (Paula, 40)

Problem number three: the scene, for many historical reasons, is organised around alcohol, drugs, cruising/casual sex and loud music. Many women thoroughly enjoy such hedonistic pleasures, but others do not. As 49-year-old Pippa stresses, this is just as true of the straight club scene:

> "I'm not one of these women who can, you know... We have a bar in Glasgow which is ladies only, and one girl said to me, that's a wonderful place to go for a quick jump, and I thought, a quick jump is something I can well do without! ... I find it very difficult. I'm sort of adrift. I'm not a person who can fit into the scene. There are aspects of it that I don't like, but then there were aspects of that social life as a wife that I didn't like either." (Pippa, 49)

The difference being that heterosexuals have a much wider range of activities open to them if clubbing is not for them!

Problem number four: lesbians are not very wealthy and there aren't enough of us around to support luxurious leisure facilities. Where the lesbian community is small and strapped for resources, the scene can be alarmingly basic:

> "I started to find women's groups, lesbian groups in my area. I live in the middle of Wiltshire and I rang up the lesbian place and they did a once-a-month women's disco. And, oh dear, that was awful. In the back of a pub, very spit and sawdust; it was absolutely horrendous." (April, 25)

Because of the pressures of homophobia, the local lesbian scene in smaller towns can develop a seige mentality. Even in a more cosmopolitan city, like Manchester, it can be a mixed blessing. The pressures to dress and behave in particular ways can sometimes be very alienating. For newly out lesbians, a particularly narrow-minded scene can be a very unfriendly place indeed:

> "I have got a really big thing about gay society; I just don't like being around a lot of gay people... It makes me feel very uncomfortable, I don't know why it is. I used to live in Manchester for about two and a half years, and it's a bit of a horrible place. Because, if you don't dress in a certain way, if you don't act in a certain way, then they just ridicule you, and they want you out." (Karla, 26)

Problems such as these have an impact on all lesbians, and the scene is not to everyone's taste. However, it seems that public perceptions of lesbian life may lead to specific problems for women who are considering leaving heterosexuality behind. In particular, the kind of lesbian generally seized on by the media in its portrayal of gay life can make some women hesitate to call themselves lesbians. If they don't measure up to the stereotype of what a lesbian looks like, they may doubt their own lesbian identity. As Catherine (40) explains:

> "I was very naive, really. Because I didn't have any urge to shave my head or be a stereotypical [lesbian]. I'm really girlie, I love dresses and lipstick and shopping! I was a real 'ladies who lunch' woman, because my

> husband was really wealthy, and so I didn't equate myself in any way with the stereotypical women out there." (Catherine, 40)

Worse, many women recounted that their lesbian community tried to reject or exclude them, either because they didn't 'look gay' or because they admitted to previous heterosexual relationships. Catherine, for example, went on to say:

> "I still actually find that hard because, even when I come here, to First Out, or go to the other bars, they say, you don't even look gay, and you think, oh, should I? I haven't got that bit right at all. There does seem to be a fixed way of... not behaving but looking, that's still quite stereotypical, it seems to me." (Catherine, 40)

> "Sometimes other lesbians would say that I wasn't [a lesbian] because I have been married. Some people are very strict, I know. I have had conversations on the internet and some people have been very, very rude to me. They have said how can you be a lesbian if you have been married? They have very strict criteria to their way of thinking." (April, 45)

> "Yes, I did contact the gay community. They make me feel that I don't fit in, because I have been married... Some of them are my age, but they have always been gay. I think to myself, well, you are very lucky then, aren't you? That's my attitude, different family, different attitude, and I think they are very lucky. I don't fit in at all... People are quite blunt and say, you are not really a lesbian because you have been married." (Margaret, 46)

Of course, there are reasons why lesbians may be cautious about accepting a woman who admits to previous heterosexual relationships, particularly when she is unwilling to dismiss her past life as a mistake.

Most lesbians have had to put up with having their lives and relationships trashed by the straight world at one time or another, and go to gays-only events in order not to have to deal with the ignorance of heterosexuals. But there is little point in trying to exclude previously heterosexual women. After all, only a tiny proportion of lesbians are 'gold-star dykes' who have never had sex with a man. When I asked Margaret what she thought about being told she wasn't really a lesbian, she didn't hesitate:

> "It's disappointing. And it makes me quite angry for a segment of society which the rest of society turns their back on and rejects; they are doing it to their own kind. It's not my fault I wasn't strong enough, or I wasn't in the right environment where I felt I could come out and be like them." (Margaret, 46)

Kerry (32) reported that, "I have found a lot more hostility from gay women when I say I've slept with men than I ever had with my straight friends or family when I came out to them." Perhaps some individuals in the heterosexual majority are simply secure enough in their own sexuality not to be threatened by the sexual choices of others. This may be far less easy for those who do not have the luxury of basking in societal approval and whose own sexual identity is hard-won. Nevertheless, it is hard to excuse lesbians who behave with such antagonism to other lesbians. Nor is it helpful when lesbian communities insist that men are all bad and lesbian relationships are beyond criticism. One woman described coming up against a particularly unhelpful attitude:

> "I got out of quite an abusive relationship with this lesbian and arrived in Bristol and met a lot of lesbians who said, well, of course, it's better to give up men because they are violent and abusive. And I thought, hang on a minute! If anything was going to make me go right back to men, it was this." (Louise, 38)

For Anna, her fears of rejection by judgemental lesbians prevented her for a long time from coming out at all. She continues to be concerned at the impact of these judgemental attitudes on vulnerable women who may be questioning their sexuality:

> "I think, as far back as I can remember, I have always had this thing that I'm really a lesbian but I'm not allowed to be a lesbian, because I'm not good enough to be a lesbian and the lesby police are going to get me, because I've slept with loads of men in the past. I've made my life choice, and now I'm not going to be allowed to change. That's how I felt, believe it or not, and it suddenly occurred to me that I could do what I liked. If I wanted to go out on the gay scene, then that was up to me, and nobody was going to stop me.
>
> "I have had a few negative reactions which were what I feared. Only one really: this woman who worked for Lesbian Line, which is really radical... Well, I think it's weird, because if anybody is ringing up Lesbian Line saying, I'm confused about my sexuality... If they are and they are told they are not allowed to be bisexual! Surely those women must go through a bisexual stage before they are identified as lesbians? And if Lesbian Line are saying they are not allowed, then they are just going to stay like I was forever, thinking, well, I want to be on the gay scene, but I am not allowed." (Anna, 35)

It feels important at this point to stress that this kind of hostility is not an inevitable response of established lesbians. Some women were at pains to emphasise that they had been welcomed and supported by other lesbians, even when they themselves were worried about what response they could expect:

> "I was fairly old, so I was quite wary about how true lesbians would receive me, because you can get people saying that if you don't know that you are gay straight

> away then you can't be. But I think I have been lucky, because my one serious girlfriend was a bit similar in that [history]. I have met women on a casual basis, like L&G societies, so that I am aware that attitude exists." (Jennie, 29)

> "I think I've been lucky in the few lesbians that I do know, in that they have been very supportive. You read a lot of books about them being very bitchy and so on, but I haven't come across any who have been like that to me. They have all been very friendly to me." (Jill, 51)

In the end, most newly out lesbians who manage to unearth their local lesbian community reach some form of love–hate relationship with the scene. As Catherine concludes, "It's that horrible thing: how do you meet people if you don't get in the scene? It's like a vicious circle. Once you have met someone you can opt out of the scene but I think you have to get into the scene to meet someone, and then you can opt out."

The big bad world

If other lesbians can be hard to track down, and not necessarily that welcoming once you have found them, what about the wider world? Again, women reported a mix of experiences. Yes, there was homophobia and discrimination, but there was also support and genuine interest. For those women whose religious beliefs were important to them, even the reaction of their church community was not always what you might imagine. Much depends on which church is involved. Some, such as the Society of Friends (Quakers) are more tolerant than others:

> "When we moved... I changed my church and walked in as this mother of three with a clean slate and... I actually said that I am a lesbian and these are my children, so I

> started right off, right from the beginning, to anyone that talked to me." (Zara, 39)

Other denominations continue to be intolerant and homophobic. The homophobia of the Catholic church, for example, prompted Liz to leave:

> "My religion; well, actually I've changed my religion. I'm not a Christian any longer. I'm a Buddhist, so I've changed that. I'm studying religion as part of my degree... I did my dissertation on homosexuality in the church, so I've done a lot of reading myself, about where attitudes originate from, but I've no time for the Catholic church now. I just don't want to know. How could I possibly want to know a church that doesn't want me to be myself? I have been repressed enough all my life, and there is no way I would put up with that now. So, when I realised, it was a complete change. All my belief systems just went out the window, everything." (Liz, 42)

Some deal with the conflict between their sexuality and their religious beliefs by choosing a more congenial religion. Others may remain within the broad Christian church, but seek out gay or gay-friendly congregations. For Louise, the experience of attending a service that (literally) spoke her language was very moving:

> "This priest said, 'We pray for queers, poofs, trannies' – and the language! And I was thinking, this is a church, and it was really powerful, and it made me cry... I just don't dare to believe yet that there is a god that loves us so much. Could there be a god that loves dykes, trannies and poofs as much as anyone else?" (Louise, 38)

But for others, whose church is unable to offer the support they need, leaving is the only option:

> "It just isn't possible to have a non-heterosexual life in the Salvation Army, and certainly not be out about it. It's coming round now; there is a thing called the Gay Salvationist Movement, but it wasn't there when I was in it." (Hilary, 40)

Religious groups and organisations are not alone in discriminating against lesbians and gay men. True, the very nature of organised religion means that it is likely to represent more conservative and backward-thinking views. Nevertheless, its prejudices reflect those that are widely held in the mainstream, and women who adopt a lesbian identity are likely to encounter such prejudices at some point. For some, this means confronting the attitudes of their community of origin:

> "... I was living in the West Indies, where you don't have any gay nightlife... What they do to gay people over there is make little images of them and stick nails in them." (Kaz, 41)

These attitudes, together with the hard work of bringing up her twins, prevented Kaz from coming out for many years. Once women do come out, they find themselves having to learn how to recognise and cope with discrimination:

> "Being gay, even now, there are certain things you cannot do, like working with children, being a mother... People think you are going to mess around with a child's head." (Karla, 26)

> "I think I experienced my first bit of discrimination yesterday, actually. I went for a job on Monday and the job was practically given to me, I was the right person and everything else. Well, somebody I know works there as well and happened to mention that I had a girlfriend and I went in yesterday for the second interview and the

> woman's attitude was totally different, and I felt that I was being pushed from the job... So much for equal opportunities." (Charlotte, 30)

Discrimination in the workplace, as encountered by Karla and Charlotte, can have serious consequences. British employment legislation has never recognised sexual orientation, despite plenty of evidence that workplace discrimination exists. European human rights legislation does now protect the employment rights of lesbians.[1] However, although the situation described by Charlotte sounds like a clear case, there is little that would stand up in a courtroom. As Charlotte herself concludes, anti-lesbian prejudice is both ill-defined and all-pervasive. It is rather like the weather, in that it touches almost every aspect of our lives:

> "I don't like being singled out, I don't like being looked at. It would be nice to be able to walk along the street holding hands without being stared at. It would be nice to get married. We are looking into having a blessing now, but it's hard." (Charlotte, 30)

For some women, not surprisingly, the experience of living in their own personal rainstorm is enough to make them wish to be straight. I met Catherine in First Out, London's popular gay coffee-bar, and she spoke with great poignancy about the sensation of looking out at an unfriendly world from inside this little haven of safety:

> "I didn't want to be [gay]. I'd rather not be. I think, if I had the option, I think it would be better to be the norm, for my kids. I'm not sad about it, yet I think most people who are in here, if they had the choice, I think they would rather be like everybody out there and there is always a slight worry when you leave here, you know. Nobody I have told has been shocked. Some people have been surprised, but nobody has said, I never want to speak to you again. But there is an element inside

> [me] that thinks it's not going to be an easy life." (Catherine, 40)

As with every other aspect of coming out, women had very different experiences of discrimination. Like Catherine, many were very aware that, in leaving heterosexuality, they had opted for a more difficult life. Sometimes lesbian life can feel like a siege situation! On the other hand, when you anticipate problems, it can be a pleasant surprise when your fears are not realised. Margaret, who had been a foster carer for many years, was concerned about the possibility that social services might regard her as no longer suitable to care for children, but her fears proved groundless:

> "The first thing I had to really sit down and talk about was who to tell and who not to tell. Then I thought social services had got to know, because I did not want them finding out in a roundabout way. Fortunately, they had just sent out this load of bumpf on fostering, and it was in the Statement of Aims. It was saying that anyone can foster, whatever your sexual orientation... So I rang up my social worker, who I am friendly with; I have known her a long time and we get on very well together... and she came and I told her and she said it makes no difference at all, absolutely none." (Margaret, 53)

Similarly, George, who runs a business with her partner teaching swimming to young children, was warned by her partner's sister-in-law that they would lose business if their sexuality became too obvious. In fact, they found exactly the opposite!

> "[There are] women locally, who think they know about us, but don't and we haven't told them. They are sort of fascinated, which makes you wonder! Because the whole town thinks it knows, we are inundated with calls. Everybody wants to come, and you can see they are fascinated! This is women; you get the odd dad turn up

> but the majority of women are fascinated... We don't fit into what they expect lesbians to fit into, you see." (George, 41)

There can be no hard and fast rules about coming out, and there is no magic formula which will work for every woman. However, one thing which does seem to be the case is that the more confident and unapologetic women were able to be, the less grief they got from friends and workmates:

> "I am completely out to my family and friends and work colleagues. Actually, it was OK because, in nursing, you meet such a wide variety of people in your work, you can't really judge people... They have been really good, just taken it in their stride. In fact they have been more supportive than the gay community." (Margaret, 46)

Conclusion: happy ever after?

On the whole, these newly out lesbians found less hostility and discrimination than might be expected. Adjusting to a way of life that you know is held in contempt by many is bound to cause anxiety, and fears about prejudice are well founded. It seems, however, that trouble may not necessarily lurk in expected places. Indeed, most of the upsetting stories came from women who had been let down by those closest to them. Parents turned out to be at the bottom of many, if not most, unhappy experiences.

This is not unusual. Parents are famous for their ability to mess with the heads of their adult offspring. They are the people who know us inside out and who know exactly how to target our weak spots. They also care deeply about our wellbeing (although it doesn't always seem that way!). Accurate information about homosexuality is not easy to get hold of, and this leaves most parents with little to fall back on when their daughter suddenly announces that she is a lesbian. Fears for her happiness, guilt about being implicated in somehow 'causing' this situation, worry about what the neighbours will say, all these can come out in angry and cruel ways. If your parents are giving you a hard time, it is reassuring to know that most of them just need time to adjust, and that they do seem to come round in the end. Sadly, of course, some parents don't. And some manage to cause a fair amount of emotional damage and family turmoil while they are 'adjusting'. There are reasons why coming out to your mum and dad is something that many lesbians just keep on putting off.

One of the saddest things to emerge from these stories is the lack of support offered by the lesbian community. New lesbians are brave women who have taken many risks and overcome many obstacles in order to come out. They both need and deserve the support of other lesbians. Sometimes that is exactly what they get. Sadly, however, lesbian communities in some areas are more likely to be judgemental, to reject and exclude women, or to be critical of their life choices. Surely, by now, we can do better than that?

Women do survive this journey. And, despite it all, most agree that it is well worth it. I would like to close this chapter with the words of Lesley, a 30-year-old mother:

> "I had someone ask me the other day: if there was a psychotherapy treatment or a pill that you could take to make you become normal would you want that? And I said no, I want to be with a woman. I know what the Bible says; I'm aware of what society says, fully aware. But I know how I feel and I know that nothing feels more right than that." (Lesley, 30)

Ashtray, corkscrew, woman: Michelle's story

"I have no idea what to call myself," starts Michelle, pondering on the truth of her sexual self. Strange that this most deliberate and determined of women should retain so much uncertainty. Yet, as she told me about her life, it became gradually clear why it was still so difficult for her to lay claim to the certainty of a label. We met in a quiet corner of a pub in a small English town. Fake 'olde worlde' decor – blackened beams and imitation bottle-glass windows – had been rendered 'fashionable' by applying a thick layer of unpleasantly 'distressed' paintwork in the kind of colours guaranteed to induce nausea in the most hardened drinker. I think it was meant to look Mediterranean.

Michelle had escaped from the office where she worked, giving up her precious lunch-hour to answer my questions. By the time she left to get back to the grindstone, I found myself full of respect for the resilient way she was trying to make sense of two conflicting pulls in her life: her sexuality and her religion. Confronted by a church which still manages to make a gospel of love and acceptance the excuse for hate and bigotry, hers is a struggle that too many lesbians (and gay men) still have to face. It seems important to let Michelle explain her struggle here.

*

I have no idea what to call myself. I suppose I am happiest with 'gay' or 'lesbian', but technically I am probably bisexual, because I have been in relationships with men and occasionally the odd one or two guys will catch my eye. But I am primarily attracted to women. Saying 'bisexual' is kind of sitting on the fence, not making up your mind, not wanting to belong to any particular camp. So, if I had to choose, I would describe myself as gay.

I always knew there was something odd about me. When I was 18, I discovered what it was. That's when I went to university. When I went to university I was going to do three things. My three things were: to buy an ashtray and use it when I liked, to buy a corkscrew and use it when I liked, and the other was to sleep with a woman. I achieved all three, actually. I had always wondered – because I'd not had any experience with women before that – when it came to the crunch whether I would find I was straight and really couldn't do it. But waking up in the morning afterwards I thought, no, it's OK. It was good!

All those things had been forbidden. My parents don't smoke. They do drink, but they don't approve of drinking to excess, and they certainly don't approve of my sexuality. Perhaps the first two are fairly flippant. It was the idea of being able to do it when I wanted and not having to sneak around. But the third was always something that I wanted to explore, and that I knew was probably more *me* than heterosexuality was.

Right from when I was eight I had a different view of my female classmates than anybody else did. I suddenly worked this out and I spent a while wondering if this was your standard childhood crush. I was aware enough of the fact that this happened to wonder if it was a passing phase. But I discovered it wasn't!

There were a couple of boyfriends, most of whom were wet drips. I went to an all-girls school, which means I only ever had my friends' version of their relationships, and I think in some way that contributed to my sexuality, because I always had the idea that men are bastards. And still do. But the only socially acceptable people to be close to were of the opposite sex. Also it was a way of testing the water, just in case I was wrong and in case these guys actually did do something for me. They didn't.

So the interim period between that realisation and going to university was very difficult. I come from a Christian background, I am a Christian myself, and it is very difficult reconciling the world where my head and psychology were leading me with what my family, my church and my Christian friends said. I knew what my beliefs said about me, and it was quite difficult. I ended up compartmentalising a lot. Church was for Sundays, and I could behave like a good Christian girl on a Sunday and in the evening my head was going other places.

At university, I decided that I was going to abandon my faith for a bit and see if I could cope. I decided to be gay and stuff the whole faith thing. But I wasn't very happy with that, and probably still wouldn't be if I made that decision again, because my faith is part of who I am. I was never happy as a secular person. I was never happy without a faith. There was always a part of me missing; it's like chopping an arm off I suppose. So, in the beginning of my third year, I made the decision to chop the other arm off and just be straight, and that didn't work either, because I fell in love with a woman. That never helps!

It didn't last. She was straight, although you wouldn't know it. In her case it was kind of a 'gay till graduation' thing. We spent most of the third year together. Our friends knew about it but neither of our parents knew about it. She was quite happy until she had to go home at the end of the year when she finished her degree. I have not been allowed to contact her, ring her, write to her or anything since then, which is quite interesting. I'm not over her and I don't expect ever to be over her.

When I came back home from university, I again decided to be straight. That didn't work either; not because there was anybody in particular but because I felt again that there was a part of me missing. So I have got up to the point where both arms are there. This happened because – and this sounds dreadfully cheesy – I went away to a Christian conference last Easter and decided that, whatever the Church thought of homosexuality wasn't actually correct. God thinks something different, and it's not the only part of my personality that counts, and he is in control; he will do it.

I am quite happy being single. I do believe that being gay is not wrong but, and this is very controversial, I do believe that *acting* gay, being in a gay relationship might be wrong. I am very much a work in progress, I think, but I am happy-ish. I have reconciled the two. I am not in touch with anybody in the Lesbian and Gay Christian Movement. I ought to be, but I am not. I never quite get the courage up to write to anybody. In a few years' time, when I leave home, I shall probably go and join a minority interest church, but I won't tell my mother what it is.

My parents are quite active in the Church. The Church is a big part of their lives and I think they believe the same things as the Church does. I think, by now, I have got enough of the 'fuck you' mentality not to worry too much about what the rest of the world thinks. But I think it would be very difficult to act out my sexuality and tell my parents about it. If it is important enough, I can, and will, but I have never found anyone with whom it is important enough.

I have to believe that it's partly genetic, because otherwise I couldn't believe that God created me the way I am. I would have to think that at some point it had all gone horribly wrong, which I don't think is true. I think God created me and loves me. I don't know, though. I've had enough experience with straight women who aren't *that* straight to know that maybe there is a part of it in everybody, suppressed or not, but I don't know.

I personally believe that, with God, all things are possible, not that all things are probable, and I fully expect my future to be me and two cats or dogs. I am not expecting to be in any relationship at all. On one level, it would be great, but on a different level, it would be very difficult to explain to my parents. It all comes back to my parents! I have to be careful how many gay-interest programmes I watch, in case they catch on to the fact that I watch them all. They get very upset and start shouting at the TV. I can feel the air bristling and you can see they just want to change channels and not be confronted with it at all.

They would certainly throw me out of the family... They would find it very difficult to love me because both of them, particularly my mother, would automatically assume that she had gone wrong somewhere, and how dare I put her in that position.

I resolutely don't think about the future, actually. I try and cope with today. It feels like I am waiting for my life to start, which it will do once I can move away.

Notes

1. For up-to-date information and advice, contact Stonewall (details in the resources section at the end of the book).

5

WAS I BORN OR DID I CHOOSE? THE ORIGINS DEBATE

> *"A lot of gay women I know have certainly always been gay. They have never slept with a bloke and wouldn't consider it. I do reckon there is a gay gene, I've got no doubts about it. For me, it just happened. Maybe the more you dabble, the more confused or freed up you get. I don't quite know how it works, but you can look at family genetics and stuff like that. What made me open to women in the first place? There are other gay members of the family, but I don't know how much of that applies to me. It doesn't really work like that for me. I just fell in love with a woman. It just happened, and it felt really nice and natural and close." (Kerry, 32)*

So, what was going through your head as you read Kerry's words? Did you seize on her certainty when she said, "I reckon there is a gay gene. I've got no doubts about it"? When you reached the part where she describes falling in love with a woman as something that "just happened" and tells us it felt "really nice and natural", did you think, "Well, yes, of course it happened and felt *natural*, because you were a lesbian all along"?

This is probably how most people would interpret Kerry's account. Here is a woman who, having been forced to conceal her true lesbian self behind a heterosexual mask, has finally recognised who she really is, and come out as a lesbian. But such a simplistic interpretation can only be made to work by choosing to ignore some important elements in what she says. For example, what are we to make of her suggestion that, "Maybe the more you dabble the more confused or freed up you get"? In short, although she has had sexual relationships with women and men and has decided that she very much prefers women, it still feels as if her sexual *identity* is either "confused" or "freed up". At the beginning of her interview she defined herself, not as a lesbian, but as "more gay than bisexual".

It is also important to remember that, when Kerry says so clearly that she believes there is a "gay gene", she is thinking about *other* lesbians, not herself. Although there are other gay members of her family, she remains unconvinced that these genetic theories make sense of her experience: "I don't know how much of that applies to me." In fact, she seems fairly certain that her life is *not* governed by a "gay gene". Having briefly considered whether it might apply to her and her family, she concludes that the answer is no: "It doesn't really work like that for me."

One of the reasons why I carried out this research was to find out how women made sense of all the theories about sexual orientation in the light of their own experiences. After all, most of the existing theories would mean that this group of women shouldn't really exist at all. Yet exist they most certainly do. So let's start by taking a slightly suspicious look at the major 'scientific' theories that claim to be able to explain homosexuality. This will involve a swift excursion through history, followed by a sideways trip into medical science. But be patient! All will make sense in the end.

It's all in the genes. And the brain. Oh yes, and the hormones

The idea that you can divide humanity up into distinct groups – homosexual, heterosexual and bisexual – is fairly new. Before the nineteenth century, it was generally thought that any one of us might experience such desires. For some cultures – such as the ancient Greeks

– this was not a particularly important issue. For others, especially those governed according to the tenets of Islam, Judaism or Christianity, desire for a member of one's own sex was thought to be sinful.[1] Anyone acting on such desires was punished, as is still the case today, for instance, in states that follow Islamic law.

So what changed in the nineteenth century? Put simply, science was rising to power and rapidly replacing religion as the preferred way of making sense of the world. In particular, scientists were busy classifying everything. This was the time when every self-respecting Victorian gentleman had his collection of specimens from the natural world, carefully mounted and labelled. Any living creature that kept still for too long risked being killed, preserved, labelled and stuck in a glass case. The risk was just as great for people. Of course, people were seldom killed for scientific purposes (although this was not unknown), but they were certainly labelled.

We are more sceptical now, but in those days scientists believed they could solve all the world's problems. Among the 'problems' they thought needed solving were lunacy, criminality, poverty and – you've guessed – sexual deviance. Middle-class Victorian men regarded most sexual behaviours as deviant, and scientists set about classifying them with the same kind of obsessive drive they had applied to fossils or butterflies. Each behaviour had to have its own name, and this name became associated with the people who enjoyed it. Just as someone who committed a crime became *a criminal*, so someone who enjoyed masturbation became an 'onanist'. Those who enjoyed or even preferred making love with members of their own sex became homosexuals. Here *homo* means 'same' (as in homogeneous), not 'man' (as in *homo sapiens*). The word 'heterosexual' was invented later, as it didn't occur to anyone at the time to classify people who were just 'normal'.

Humanity had been divided up into two distinct groups. This caused problems that we are still grappling with today. Firstly, they soon found that it didn't work. Too many people seemed to belong in both groups, or moved from one to the other. The notion of bisexuality was invented to account for such people; this was, indeed, the only way of ensuring that the whole system didn't simply collapse.

As we shall see, the idea of bisexuality continues to perform this function for women struggling to make their experiences fit into this nineteenth-century framework.

Secondly, having decided that homosexuality was a condition, scientists had to find evidence that this was so. So far all their efforts have produced rather dismally weak results, but this has not stopped each new theory being greeted with great excitement. Clearly the world *really* wants an explanation for this strange behaviour!

The third problem is the one that has had the greatest impact on lesbians (and gay men). Although the categories *homosexual*, *heterosexual* and *bisexual* are supposed to explain erotic desire, what they are based on is not desire at all, but biological sex – maleness and femaleness. Once you begin to think along these lines, you end up in a rather strange place! According to this way of thinking, it is normal for a man to desire a woman, but abnormal for him to desire a man. It is also normal for a woman to desire a man, but abnormal for her to desire a woman. Therefore, the sex of the person you are attracted to becomes immensely important. It defines *the kind of person* you are. Maleness starts to mean 'desires women' and femaleness starts to mean 'desires men'.

Of course, if this is the case, then anyone who desires woman is demonstrating some kind of maleness, and anyone who desires men is demonstrating some kind of femaleness. Following this empty logic to its conclusion, lesbians are masculine and gay men are effeminate. Of course, if a masculine person desires another masculine person, they must be effeminate... which means that lesbians are really gay men and gay men are really lesbians. Which explains a lot about some close friends of mine, but doesn't look good as the basis for scientific research!

Nevertheless, this idea of the masculine lesbian and the girlish gay man soon became the dominant explanation for homosexuality. It is called the 'sexual inversion model' and it underpins all 'scientific' research into lesbian or gay sexuality.

The sexual inversion model, first given that name by John Addington Symonds, dominated the thinking of sexologists from the second half of the nineteenth century onwards. It has also been very influential in mainstream culture, where the stereotypical 'bulldagger' lesbian has long been held up to derision. As we shall see, the prevalence of this idea continues to cause confusion and anxiety among women questioning their desires.

Belief in sexual inversion means that biomedical research into homosexuality has concentrated on looking for signs of femaleness in gay men's bodies and (much less frequently) for signs of maleness in lesbians' bodies. As scientific technology has advanced, so researchers have used more sophisticated techniques in their increasingly desperate search for symptoms of homosexuality.[2] In the 1930s and 40s, researchers measured the bodies of lesbians and gay men using very crude instruments. For example, vaginal depth was measured using a researcher's finger. Once the finger was as far in as it would go, a piece of wire was wound round at the point where it vanished into the woman! The idea behind such silliness is that a lesbian, not being a proper woman, would have smaller 'female parts' (vagina, womb, pelvis) than a heterosexual woman. Although, since she undoubtedly took the 'male role' in lovemaking, she would have a larger clitoris!

Today there are three competing theories which claim to have established a biological basis for homosexuality.[3] Gunter Dorner and John Money claim it is hormonal in origin – that the little lesbian foetus receives too strong a dose of 'male' hormones while still in her mother's womb. Simon LeVay claims that a tiny component of the brain's neuroanatomy (to be precise, the third interstitial nucleus on the anterior hypothalamus) is a similiar size in gay men and straight women. Finally, Dean Hamer and his team claim that they have found "DNA markers linking homosexuality with a region on the X chromosome that boys get from their mothers".

It seems doubtful that there is any substance to any of these. For a start, they cannot all be correct since they are so very different. The fact that scientists are scrabbling round in such very different area – hormones, genes and brain anatomy – suggests that they are on a wild-goose chase. In addition, the research methods of all of them have been widely criticised. Money and Dorner's work was on rats, and cannot reasonably be the basis for any claims about people. LeVay used the brains of men who had died with AIDS – and HIV can cause serious damage to brain tissue – and decided that all the female brains he used in comparison *must* be heterosexual, because lesbians are very rare (no, seriously, this is for real!). Hamer's team, on the other hand, didn't bother checking other family members to see if they had the 'gay' gene. They didn't even check the mothers of the men in their sample.

It begins to look as if the hetero/homo divide is not quite what we think it is. Indeed most social scientists would probably now agree with lesbian sociologist Mary McIntosh, who is famous for declaring, as long ago as 1968:

> "The failure of research to answer the question... results from the fact that the wrong question has been asked. One might as well try to trace the aetiology [cause] of 'committee chairmanship' or 'Seventh Day Adventism' as of 'homosexuality'."[4]

Scientists tend not to pay much attention when told they are barking up the wrong tree, and theories about hormones, brain structure and (perhaps especially) gay genes continue to attract research funds. They also continue to grab the headlines and, in consequence, to haunt the mind of every woman who tries to make sense of her lesbian desires and identity. While heterosexuals have the luxury of never having to think about it, it is a rare lesbian who manages to avoid asking herself, "Was I born like this or did I choose? Was it something that happened to me when I was young? Have I been a lesbian all along and just never realised?"

So, does this feel like something you were born with, or is it more complicated? This was a question I asked everyone. Counting up the answers is quite interesting. Out of 80 women, 28 thought they had always been lesbians and might perhaps have been born gay. Another 35 said that their sexuality had changed, or even that it was freely and consciously chosen. The remaining 17 felt either unable or unwilling to decide between nature and nurture, and a small number of these thought it was probably a bit of both.

Let's start by listening to women who feel – some quite strongly, some more tentatively – that they have been lesbians all along.

The born (again?) lesbians

Almost every woman who spoke to me was a little hesitant about deciding between nature and nurture. A few, on the other hand, were quite certain:

> "I think it is something you are born with, something that is there, and it is just whether or not you face it. I don't think you can decide to be gay, not really *being*. You are or you are not." (Michelle, 30)

The degree of conviction expressed by Michelle was rare. It seemed to be more common for women to admit that, although they felt quite strongly that their lesbian self was their *real* self, they remained unsure about some of the explanations that have been put forward. Most were likely to agree with Jill who, at 51, had worked very hard at heterosexual life. Still finding herself unhappy despite her best efforts, she is drawn to the 'nature' side of the argument but finds the existing theories inadequate:

> "I think it is probably something I was born with. Although I don't know why I should have been. There's no one else in my family, or anything like that. I don't think it can be in your genes. I don't know where it is, to be honest. I suppose it's hormonal. I don't know." (Jill, 51)

For women who believe that their lesbianism is an intrinsic part of who they are, the fact that they have lived heterosexual lives must be explained. After all, if lesbianism is 'natural' for them, the lives they have been living are 'unnatural'. Their heterosexuality, which they experience very much as a mistake or as being wrong for them, is put down to many things: social pressures to conform, fear of stigma, the desire for the security of normal married life, wanting to have children or simply not having any idea that there were such things as lesbians or a lesbian life.

> "I never felt safe or comfortable with men... I always felt different. At that time I wasn't aware. I didn't even know lesbians existed... When I was about twelve I remember being called 'lezzie' and things like that in the school playground, but not understanding. I think probably I would always have been gay, but never had the chance to find out, because of my childhood, and abuse. Never knowing lesbians existed. I think I've always been gay and probably should never have been out with men." (Julie, 35)

This sense of feeling *different* is vague for some, more acute for others, but always uncomfortable. It is, of course, a fairly common human experience, perhaps especially during adolescence, which is precisely the time in our lives when we are trying to establish who we are and to construct a unique identity for ourselves. For women who, in later life, start to rebuild their identity round their lesbian desires, that uncomfortable feeling begins to make sense. Indeed, the conviction that she has been a lesbian all along can be very powerful in this way. Several women commented that this recognition had helped many different elements in their lives fall into place:

> "I think I was always a lesbian but I didn't recognise it as such, and I didn't know there were options. But once I acknowledged it to myself, everything in my life made sense. And it hadn't before; nothing had made sense before. But once I thought, oh yes, now I understand, it all fell into place. Why I had always had good relationships with women, why I had always had poor relationships with men, all those whys." (Elizabeth, 45)

As we have seen, scientific attempts to explain lesbianism are flimsy, to say the least. The ideas about desire and biological sex which underpin them are naive and unsophisticated. This does not mean, however, that we can dismiss the idea that some women may, indeed, be drawn to members of their own sex from a very early age. Listening to some of these accounts, it is hard to deny that *something* seems to be present in some women's lives even though they may not want it or even recognise it:

> "I met my ex-husband when I was 15, so really I didn't have the opportunity to explore my sexuality at all... We had a good marriage, really, but we always knew that there was something not quite right. I knew there was something that wasn't right. It sounds daft, looking back. People say, how was it you didn't realise? Deep down I must have done but I had a very strict Catholic upbringing and, you know what it's like; society conditions you to go down a certain road and you do that. You get married. I've got two children as well, and so really, I didn't realise. But when I look back, I've never fantasised about a man; it's always been about women. I know it sounds daft, but it never really occurred to me. But, subconsciously, I must have realised that there was something. I suffered with depression on and off for years, and I was never really happy in myself, and I realise now that that's what it was." (Liz, 42)

A word of caution may be necessary at this point. There is no doubt that this was a life-changing experience for Liz, and one that profoundly enhanced her wellbeing. But for women who, like her, explain their lives retrospectively in this way, there are risks. It is not difficult to imagine that a woman who believes her episodes of depression were caused by repressed lesbian feelings may feel a tremendous sense of release once she is able to recognise and act on those feelings. But life is seldom as cut and dried as this, and lesbians get depressed, too. If you believe that coming out will solve all your problems you may be devastated when this turns out not to be the case.

The sense that the lesbian part of oneself is somehow intrinsic, that it is one's essential, true self, can be extremely powerful. Even sceptical academics who reject the scientific theories *intellectually* may find that they cannot dismiss them altogether:

> "My intellect tries to kick in straight away, because I am into the social construction of everything, and I don't like the notion of being programmed. However, when I look back now I can't actually think of a time when I wasn't really attracted to my own sex, women. Inside me somewhere, I know this. At six, in a way, I was as I am now. It is complicated, and I do find it difficult. I guess it *feels* genetic, and I think that is often the thing. A lot of lesbians, and perhaps even more gay men, seem to go with that; sort of 'it's the way I am, I was born that way,' because it feels, exactly, intrinsic." (Robbie, 48)

However strong this feeling is for many women, the majority of the women who took part in this study do not believe they were born gay. This is not altogether unexpected since I was not working with women who had always lived a lesbian life and had never had sex with a man. What was interesting, however, was that women who dismissed the 'nature' side of the debate and came down strongly in favour of 'nurture' generally spent more time explaining why this was so. Far from being dismissive, their replies were thoughtful and considered – if strongly worded at times! They were, however, unanimous in rejecting biological theories:

> "I don't believe them for a minute! Sometimes you suddenly think, I wonder if I ought to give this some thought. But I really can't, at a gut level, engage with them, because I think sexuality isn't an either/or. I think it's shaped from lots of different messages and experiences as you are growing up." (Grace, 47)

In common with most of the women who reject these explanations, Grace explains that sexuality seems far too complex to be fitted neatly into a biological box. Having decided this, she feels that it is more true to see it as something that evolves through our early lives. Len agrees, adding the suggestion that women who change sexuality have to have the ability to be open to experiences which go against social and cultural expectations:

> "I certainly wouldn't say that I was born one, or that it is hormonal or genetic or any of those things. When I describe my own sexuality or how I came to be, I would say it's very much on the continuum. I believe that actually most people are probably born in the middle of the continuum, bisexual, and because of society, the way that we are brought up, most people are pushed to the heterosexual side. Possibly I was just able to be more open and to look at the homosexual side and think, well, actually, this is better for me and this is my choice, that I actually prefer to be with a woman." (Len, 38)

Sally clearly thinks something similar. Although unwilling to dismiss the experiences of people who feel very differently from her, she would agree with Len's inclination to identify social pressures as a major factor at play:

> "It is complicated. Clearly, some people do feel that they were born that way, and who am I to tell them that they are wrong? That would not be on at all. But for me, it wasn't like that. So, if you ask me what I think happens, I think that biology or genes don't have anything to do with it. I think it's just what your society makes possible, and if you have the possibility then some people have strong experiences which make them want to explore. And if you like one thing more than another, well, then you go for it. I think it is as simple as that. But it has been made more complicated and more muddled because for some reason society finds it difficult. Society finds lesbian and gay people difficult. I have no idea why, because it makes no sense to me." (Sally, 46)

For a few, the whole thing was put down to chance. According to this view, accidental life events were the guiding influence. As for biological theories:

> "I think that's so much nonsense! Looking and thinking about my own story, and the accidents in my life which have allowed me to move away from the drabness of heterosexuality. I have loved men, and I have never, honestly, felt oppressed by men... But when you have lived your life in black and white, which is how many people have, living it in colour is difficult to describe!" (Virginia, 44)

Virginia feels that it was an accident that she ended up in bed with a woman and that, having once tasted the delights of lesbian love, it made little sense to return to the monochrome world of heterosexuality! This is a delightful proposal but leaves many questions unanswered. Why do some women cheerfully succumb to the prospect of lesbian seduction while others recoil in horror? Why do some women experiment with lesbian sex only to return to men? For partners Louise and Adie, questions of social conformity and early experiences cannot be left out of the picture:

> "I believe that I was heterosexual and that I had a change. But of course I was brought up to conform, so I don't know how big an influence that would have been." (Louise, 38)

> "I don't believe those genetic theories, but I do believe that our sexuality is formed by some very early experiences. There *may* be a kind of predisposition in some sense but if I had to put a percentage on it, I think that more than 80% is experience. It's socialisation, it's who we are mirrored by, and, particularly, early sexual experience." (Adie, 29)

Even when women were prepared to acknowledge that there might, indeed, be some kind of predisposition involved, they insisted that it was much less significant than social factors (such as stigma and the expectation that women would marry), psychological factors (such as early childhood experiences or a particularly liberal upbringing) or straightforward choice. For some individuals, younger and more confident generally, the element of choice felt particularly strong:

> "I always feel that I have a choice, in most areas of my life. I have argued with people that, if I had to be with men, I could do it. I wouldn't want to, and I certainly wouldn't choose to, and I probably wouldn't be as happy as I am. Maybe there is a biological element to it, but I don't feel that that's the driving thing. I think it's a decision that [for me] became clear with a certain amount of academic influence, reading, studying, and meeting women who had a lot to say on the subject." (Kate, 26)

Perhaps there is something, after all, in those right-wing fears that letting gay people become teachers might undermine traditional family values!

Some women, having rejected biological explanations for their experiences, go on to reject the assumptions that those explanations are based on. For Janine, it makes no sense any longer to divide people up into two groups:

> "I think [the genetic theory] is absolute rubbish. I really believe that I chose to be straight and I believe that, if anybody wasn't happy with their sexuality they could choose to change it. I don't believe that I was born gay, I believe that it's all part of a learning experience in life... I don't believe that we're gay or straight." (Janine, 31)

Some women, who agreed with Janine that the gay/straight split was not a useful reflection of reality, pointed out that it was used to police behaviour within the gay community, keeping people inside their little boxes:

> "I think all those sorts of statements tend to annoy me, because they just don't seem to fit. There was an article in the *Guardian* today about straight women who have affairs with lesbians, a very critical article: it said basically you are either straight or gay, don't mess around. I think any form of positiveness like that tends to annoy me because people just aren't that straightforward and aren't that simple." (Louise, 32)

If Janine and Louise are right about this, and there are no fixed and separate categories, then the whole thing is a matter of choice. For women who have struggled for years, sometimes decades, to repress their feelings of longing for sexual contact with other women, the notion that a lesbian identity can be freely chosen must seem outrageous, almost insulting. Nevertheless, some women do claim just that. Others have a lingering sense of uncertainty. It is almost as if they are asking themselves, can it *really* be that simple:

> "I've read a lot of these theories, and even my mum is upset: 'You weren't developed properly in the womb' and all this lot. When I hear people say you were born like this, and it's not a choice, well, I feel like saying, I chose this way, and to some extent I did." (Suzanne, 37)

Others, while clearly stating that they made a free choice, acknowledge that such a choice is only possible under certain circumstances. The social and psychological factors have to be supportive, or at least, not make the notion of choice completely unrealistic:

> "I think it's all social conditioning. It's a good choice for me, but it probably wouldn't have done me any harm to be happily married with three kids. It's just a choice that I was able to make now, and I made it. It was an easy

> choice to make. I wasn't in a country where you get stoned in the street. If I was, I probably wouldn't have chosen it." (Katie, 26)

Again, this is a very powerful and affirming statement but it leaves some things open. There are countries in the world today where homosexual behaviour is punishable by death, but some individuals remain undeterred. This may suggest a 'drive', in the biological sense, that is so irresistible that it overrides the threat of death. If this is the case, evolutionary theory would suggest that homosexuality would have died out by now. On the other hand, the power of romantic love coupled with sexual attraction may in itself be strong enough to make people take terrible risks. Think of Romeo and Juliet!

It is, however, unquestionable that certain women *do* choose to become lesbians. To be able to make such a choice demands certainty that you have the right to decide what to do with your own body – something routinely denied women in patriarchal cultures. We should not forget that it is still remarkable that 35-year-old Anna can say, "I believe that my sexuality is my own and I can choose how I use it." Even in relatively liberal twenty-first century Britain, most religious leaders and many politicians would beg to disagree. Moreover, biological explanations for homosexuality have become so widely believed that, as Claire says, the idea of choice confuses people. She remains unwavering. For her, this was indeed a choice:

> "Absolutely. Totally. Really explicitly. Sat down and worked out the pros and cons and decided this was what I wanted to be. That weirds people out! They can't believe that you can make such a conscious decision." (Claire, 24)

Alongside those lesbians who made a conscious choice about their sexuality we find another group. These women, whilst perhaps not signing up for any particular theory, stress the dangers of supporting a genetic explanation:

> "I think, especially with the progress of genetics nowadays, it is too dangerous to discuss. It's possible. Some friends of mine, for example, have never had any sexual relationship with a man and you could argue that they were born lesbians. I don't think so. I think it's a choice. I certainly don't think it's genetically programmed and I would oppose this point of view very strongly, from a political position if nothing else." (Gala, 45)

Claire, from a slightly different perspective, angrily rejects biological theories because she sees them as judgemental. She paints a vivid picture of her own transition, seeing it as something to do with perception and understanding. Certainly, hers is a more sophisticated approach that cannot be neatly tidied away into biology:

> "Anybody who speaks in judgement of others, whether it's a scientist or a politician, is going to anger me in a small way, and I feel that sense of anger when scientists say we can describe that particular sort of human behaviour in that particular way... I think that people are people and that circumstances change you. Maybe they don't introduce anything new to you, maybe they just show you a different side of yourself. Like a grimy window. You can be looking through the same window and someone comes along and cleans it, and you look through at something totally different; perhaps it was always there, perhaps it wasn't." (Claire, 35)

Ruth, who, at the age of 58, is one of the oldest of the group to have made a conscious choice to live as a lesbian, is also impatient with genetic explanations. She points out that, not only is the notion of choice more challenging, but the genetic argument leads to some terrifying possibilities:

> "I think it is extremely important that the idea of choice is allowed to be recognised for us, because of this

> business of, 'Oh, it is all genetic, so they can't help it, poor loves.' Whereas it is very subversive, and dangerous to [mainstream] culture, if we say, 'well, actually I made a choice.' A lot of people don't like this, to make choices. It is maybe quite subversive to say, 'Yes, I did have a choice, I could have stayed heterosexual but I didn't want to. I chose my life and I choose to stay here and not to go back.' Whereas, if it is biological and we can't help it, I think that is dangerous. That leaves us open to some unpleasant cures!" (Ruth, 58)

Ruth was not the only one worried about unpleasant cures. Florence, while not going so far as to reject the possibility that she might have been born gay, was unambiguous in rejecting any genetic theory that might result in 'something dreadful':

> "In a sense, does it matter if you were born one or became one? I am not one of those people who say you have to be born it. I just feel that, OK, this is me, this is where I am now. Yes, I think I probably was born gay, and I am quite comfortable with that thought, but I am also aware of people who are very uncomfortable with it, and the nasty right-wing political people who think, OK, if we can find the gene that makes you gay we will find the gene that makes you ungay. Thank you very much, I don't want to know that one! ... I am frightened about the way people might use that information. If there is a gay gene, I am scared that some narrow-minded, bigoted scientist is going to do something dreadful, and that is what I am really uncomfortable about. I am proud to be where I am and I wouldn't want to be anywhere else. I am absolutely and utterly happy. Couldn't dream of being anything else!" (Florence, 44)

Happy sitting on the fence

Given how much publicity the media has given to each new biological theory, and given how little interest there seems to be in the real-life experiences of real, live lesbians, it comes as no surprise that plenty of us can't quite make up our minds what we think. For some, this is a matter of not having decided yet, with the underlying assumption that they may well make up their minds at some point in the future:

> "I have often thought about is it nature versus nurture and is it genetic or whatever, and I still haven't made up my mind what I think about it." (Sue, 44)

Others are unwilling to choose nature or nurture, feeling intuitively that elements of both are at play:

> "I think there are influences at a biological level that may predispose people in a certain direction... I probably have something of that as well; but I know, for myself, I have been influenced to a certain extent just by my life experiences, which made me look a bit more towards what are the options available to me." (Jennie, 29)

Jennie has clearly thought about this complicated question and has come up with an explanation that manages to incorporate the many different factors that she feels have influenced her decision. She is not able to exclude biological, social or psychological elements, but is quite content that a mix of all of them enables her to make sense of her own life.

Many people find uncertainty difficult to live with, and this is perhaps more likely to be true where sexuality is concerned. It is, after all, something that feels very close to the core of who were are, in this sex-obsessed culture of ours. Sitting on the fence in the nature/nurture debate can appear rather confusing. We can imagine a scientist, for example, being quite unable to accept a position as ambivalent as 28-year-old Marie's. "Was I born with it?" she asks, concluding, "I think so. Although I also think it is a choice."

It is, of course, tempting to look back from the vantage point of a new lesbian identity and rewrite one's past history so that it fits in with the idea that this is something that was always there. As May (39) cautions, "I think, in hindsight, it's difficult now to make a judgement that's not clouded." She was not the only woman to express such reservations. Sue (50) was aware of the temptation to rewrite her personal history, concluding, "You could write my story one way that says I have have always been a lesbian, but that wasn't how I felt at the time."

There may be good psychological reasons for rewriting past history to confirm that one has been a lesbian all along. This is, after all, a very significant life-change, and one that tends to cause a lot of pain, disruption and hurt. Having gone through all that once, what woman in her right mind would want to contemplate doing it again in the other direction? There is also likely to be a very real need for justification. When a woman leaves an established heterosexual life, the upheaval touches many people around her: parents, husbands, siblings, friends and, most of all, children. In addition to all this personal pain, social disapproval may be felt very strongly. Which of us can go through all this without being assailed by guilt? So the idea that this is something out of the individual's conscious control, something she can neither choose nor resist, is an important safety net. It offers reassurance that she is not a bad mother, a wicked person, a selfish woman. It may also, as we have seen, offer a relatively painless way for rejected men to soothe their wounded pride, or for parents to explain their daughter's behaviour to family and friends.

It must take considerable confidence not to fall back on the justification offered by biological explanations. This kind of confidence can be heard in the words of some women, as they explain why they are just not that interested in theories, they just want to get on and enjoy life:

> "I probably will stick with women, but I think that it is foolish to assume that my sexuality is going to be the same for the next thirty or forty years. It hasn't been for the past thirty-odd years... I did have a lot of crushes on

girls when I was very young. In the Brownies, I was the mascot and I adored it. I suppose, if you looked at that, you could say that I was biologically determined to be a lesbian... But I'm not in a frame of mind to analyse, because then I think it takes some of the enjoyment out of sexual relationships. This constant analysing. I grew up in the 1960s and I think it was the perfect time for me to grow up in. A time when sex was very much up for grabs... Sleep with men, sleep with women, whatever. It doesn't matter to me that much, as it does to other people." (Barbara, 47)

If Barbara refuses to analyse the roots of her sexuality because she doesn't want to complicate her enjoyment of it, Margaret admits that she would quite like to believe in a genetic explanation, but that she simply can't make it fit her experiences. Like some of the other women we have heard speaking about this, her deliberations have led her to conclude that the dividing line between gay and straight is not as clear as we might like to think:

> "Do I believe in a gay gene? Yes and no. It's nice to think it's nature and natural, but it's not been proved. I think it is in all of us, stronger in some women than in others. Yes, I think I was probably born like it, but what puzzles me is why I am capable of enjoying sex with a man... I know I can enjoy sex with a man. It might be because I needed to [conform], but it's there. I have read about gay women having relationships with men and gay men having relationships with women. If people press the right buttons, you are capable of enjoying sex with most people. Nothing is black and white. Sexuality is really a grey area. And that is the problem, because people don't see it. You are either gay or straight and that is it." (Margaret, 46)

For some, the need to find a theory that fits is far less important than working out the best way to live their lives. When you are trying to get your sexuality to fit in with your moral, spiritual or religious beliefs, other questions may seem less significant:

> "I think it's a combination. This is something that I have read a lot about. But for me, I am not sure. It can sometimes be something, maybe genetic, maybe hormonal, that happened. There are all these theories. Or it could actually be something that happened so far back, so you feel you were born with it. But my point of view is that, based on a lot of what I believe, on my Christian faith as well, to me it's immaterial. Was I born this way, did life make me this way or was it a choice I have made? However I am born, I can choose the actions that I perform, and perhaps I can't help what I am, but I can help what I do about it. But I do feel this was perhaps part of me, long before I was ever aware of it." (Barbara, 49)

Listening to these women's voices it seems that there are many different ways of responding to the scientists who insist that they can track down the cause of our sexuality. For some, the suggestion that they have always been gay, and that this was caused by events – whether biological or in childhood – beyond their control, simply fits in best with their experiences. For other, it offers reassurance that they are not acting selfishly, or that they have reached 'home' and won't ever have to change sexuality all over again. Other women either can't make such theories match with their lives, or they reject the idea of predetermination, or they simply reckon that, sex and love being what they are, things are not as clear cut as the scientists claim.

It is, I think, important to emphasise that a small number were able simply to weigh up their options and make a rational choice to become lesbians. It needs to be stressed, given the uncomfortable history of 'political' lesbianism, that this choice was not a negative one motivated by political hatreds but a positive one, springing from self-care and a real delight in women. For yet others (and I include myself in this group), the most urgent question is not whether lesbian desires are born, made or chosen, but why scientists are trying to find a genetic explanation and what they will do if they can claim to have found it.

The process of questioning all the available explanations is one with which most heterosexuals don't have to bother. This is why most of them are so poorly equipped when someone close to them comes out. They have simply never had to inform themselves about the debates. Most lesbians, on the other hand, spend at least some time pondering the vexed question of sexual orientation. Many come out of this process equipped with extremely sophisticated ways of thinking about sexuality, and some conclude that the gay/straight boxes are perhaps not as watertight as they had been led to believe.

Bulldagger or lipstick lesbian?

As we have seen, existing theories of 'homosexuality' are all based on the assumption that lesbianism is 'caused' by some rogue element of masculinity. Either the sweet little girl baby was exposed to horrid male hormones in the womb, or she has some manly glitch on her chromosomes, or there is an alien scrap of masculine tissue in her anterior hypothalamus.

It is not difficult to demolish these theories academically, but they have been enormously influential. For most of the last century, doctors believed that they would be able to spot their lesbian patients by their enormous clitorises, hairy chests and gruff voices. There are documented instances where such beliefs led to malpractice or negligent treatment of lesbians.[5] They have also been influential among lesbians, and it is fascinating to hear how the myth of the manly lesbian continues to have an impact on women today:

> "I've met women who have said, oh no, I wanted to be a boy, or I was wearing this or that. I was your typical girl: wear Mum's heels, and Barbies, and dolls' prams, and lipstick at 13. I never felt anything masculine about me at all" (Suzanne, 37)

Suzanne had clearly experienced some uncertainty from other lesbians, who had internalised the notion that lesbian equals masculine. Happily, she has been able to resolve this with the aid of a relatively new label, that of 'lipstick lesbian':

> "I mean, I class myself as a very feminine woman. I still like to wear skirts and makeup, and some of the women find that a bit strange. They seemed to have this uniform when I came out: you had to wear certain things. And I found that hard, because I like to wear... Well, if you passed me in the street I would look like an ordinary straight woman. I don't have a shaved head or anything. I class myself as a lipstick lesbian." (Suzanne, 37)

Heterosexual friends and family members can be just as strongly influenced by the masculinity myth as any lesbian:

> "One of my sister-in-laws said, when I first went up to London, don't cut all your hair off, don't wear dungarees and don't drink beer out of a bottle! So I go back every now and again and say, look, no dungarees, no beer out of a bottle!" (April, 45)

Clearly, April was quite able to educate her sister-in-law out of her belief in these stereotypes. Some women, however, find it difficult to question received wisdom, and may actually hold back from coming out in consequence:

> "I had some preconceived ideas what a lesbian was, and I think that had a large influence on how I dismissed my sexuality. One of the preconceived ideas was that [being] a lesbian was somehow connected to a gender thing. You know, if you feel you are a woman then you can't possibly be a lesbian – which sounds mad, but I did have these preconceived ideas. I am fully a woman, so at that time I didn't see how I could possibly be a lesbian!" (Theresa, 35)

In complete contrast to Theresa, of course, many women point to their lack of femininity as evidence of lesbianism. In particular, if a lesbian remembers being a tomboy in childhood, she is likely to identify that as early evidence of her sexuality:

> "All the strong indicators are there. Sporting kid's life, tomboyish, doing all the physical stuff with Dad... I certainly wasn't brought up as a 'girlie' girl... I think my tomboy lifestyle was very comfortable, very me. I look odd in skirts and dresses, I am happy in my jeans and trousers and trainers." (Nicky, 38)

However, for every lesbian who can lay claim to a tomboy streak, there is another with rather different memories:

> "I am very bad at being a tomboy! I had two very close boy friends who lived next door to me when I was younger, and so I joined in all the climbing trees and building dens and whatever, but I didn't do it very well. I would never have described myself as a tomboy. I didn't like dresses, because I didn't like my legs." (Katie, 23)

Even though Nicky sees her tomboy actions as 'strong indicators', she stresses that this does not extend (as the theories insist that it must) into the bedroom or the relationship with her girlfriend:

> "But there is no [masculinity] to do with sex and sexuality, no. I mean, I am more likely to wire a plug and stuff like that, and I do moan at women who do not know how to change a light bulb... But then I haven't got a clue where the oil goes in my car, but my girlfriend does. She is more feminine than me, but sexually we between us have a very equal... It swings within conversation, it swings within us making love." (Nicky, 35)

This is a very important issue, because tomboy behaviour is so widely used within medical science to 'prove' theories about lesbianism, gender identity dysphoria and a host of other ways in which people refuse to conform to gender regulations. So I asked a group of heterosexual women, who had never been lesbians or experimented with lesbian sex, whether they remembered being tomboys at all. According to the theories, the answer should be no. In fact, the proportion of heterosexual women who recalled being tomboys was *greater* than the proportion of lesbians. This can't be used to prove anything, partly because the number I spoke to was smaller (20 heterosexuals, as opposed to 80 lesbians), but it makes it very difficult to argue that tomboyishness in childhood can be associated with lesbianism in adult life.

Indeed, some women related that becoming lesbians had enabled them to relax more about being feminine. For these women, leaving heterosexuality and its assumptions behind had allowed them to become *more* womanly rather than less so:

> "I identified more with the boys and was very tomboyish, which totally upset my mum. And living up trees and playing football was great, until they decided that they couldn't really be seen with girls, so I was thrown out of the group... So a few years ago, before I came out, if I'd thought about lesbians I'd have said yes, it was because of the slightly more masculine side [of me]. But it freed my feminine side. I had denied my feminine side. I wouldn't wear feminine colours, I hated skirts and dresses; as a heterosexual woman I was a very masculine one! I made my own way in the world and I was going to sort stuff out and I was in charge. And I didn't like being a woman. But since I have been able to accept my identity as a gay woman, I wear pink, I sometimes wear skirts and I am more comfortable in them. And I really like being a woman. It's a grand place to be!" (Zara, 39)

The idea that a woman might become *more* feminine once she stopped having relationships with men and started living as a lesbian should make us chuck all the biological nonsense out of the window. But what might it mean? Why would this happen? Julie has a very similar story, and she also suggests what might lie behind this unexpected experience. For women to try and achieve an equal relationship with men, she explains, involves a lot of competition and challenge:

> "When I was straight, I remember really competing with men. But that was until I did a degree. I wasn't very articulate, I couldn't actually say what I thought. I think my competition with men [was because] I always wanted to be on equal status with them. I didn't want to be treated as a girl, someone who couldn't sort the car out or wasn't able to put shelves up. I was always competing with the male partners I had. I always wanted to be treated equally, and not be regarded as the person who did the washing up and the cooking. I always used to resent that!
>
> "It wasn't until I became gay that I actually went, no, I can't sort the car out, I'll take it to a garage. I could then go, no, I'm a girl, if I don't know something I'll go ask somebody. Whereas, before, I would always go, if I don't know something I've got to know, I've got to be independent. [As a lesbian] I became more relaxed and enjoyed being female more. I wore more female clothes, I was more effeminate, I could say, yes, I like cooking... I just felt real, I just felt me, I didn't have to pretend any more." (Julie, 35)

Sally pinpoints something similar:

> "Well, I think, with my husband, it was always some kind of fight to prove who wore the trousers, just to teach him women weren't pathetic creatures. But that was marriage, which is a whole weird world; you don't have to do that with another woman. It's not at issue, it would be just silly. What would be the point? And also, when you are

> a lesbian it suddenly becomes really daring and unconventional to wear a dress. Other dykes are shocked, they disapprove, and heterosexuals are really, but *really* confused. So, of course, I do!" (Sally, 44)

Other lesbians, whilst they did not recall having become *more* feminine once they came out, stressed that, as far as they were concerned, being a lesbian was interwoven with a deep pleasure and sense of pride in being a woman. Often, when explaining such feelings, they stressed the physical powers and capacities of women's bodies:

> "I loved my female body and I loved my menstrual cycle; I thought it was wonderful... Yes, yes, I love my female sexuality. And it's absolutely amazing that women can give birth! I think that is a whole [explanation] for patriarchy, because men are completely miffed because they can't give birth. But I think my body is just incredible. I would love to have loads of children." (Anna, 35)

> "I have never, *never* thought that I didn't want to be a woman. I have always been happy and proud to be a woman, and pleased to be a woman, and I have always found the idea of women wanting to be men puzzling. Except in the sense of wanting to have power and status and so on." (Sue, 50)

Sue's thoughtful way of distinguishing between physiology and social issues probably hints at something significant. After all, it is not that long ago that medical scientists identified an interest in science as a likely symptom of lesbianism! Issues that are clearly social or cultural – such as the belief that science is a male activity – have an enormously powerful effect on individual women's lives and personalities. Yet such factors are just not taken seriously by certain scientists (and, intriguingly, they are almost exclusively men) who claim that biology explains desire. Perhaps scientists need to get out more!

Conclusion

The point here is not to prove or disprove theories, rather, it is to explore the impact of those theories on the lives of women as they come out, and to assess whether the impact is generally negative or positive. Of course, the answer is, both. There is no doubt that some women find the idea that they are fixed in their lesbian identity very comforting and helpful. Other women feel equally strongly that biological explanations fail to make sense of their lives and may even be dangerous. Some of the political implications of this debate are addressed in the final chapter.

Here I would just like to stress two things. Firstly, there is precious little evidence for the claim that lesbians are in some way masculinised. Indeed, rather the opposite seems to be the case. Not only do many non-lesbian women recall tomboy childhoods, but lesbians themselves seem perfectly able to be as butch or as girlie as they please. It seems likely that conformity or resistance to one's feminine role has more to do with personality, politics and socialisation than anything else.

Secondly, many women who chew over the nature/nurture debate conclude that they don't much care one way or the other. This may be because they have better things to do, like getting on with the pains and pleasures of living a lesbian life. Or it may be because the question makes so little sense that they end up thinking that the dividing line between gay and straight isn't really there at all.

Something said by Virginia sums this up beautifully. Having rejected genetic explanations as "so much nonsense", she went on to muse, reflectively, on the women she saw around her in the everyday world. Was there any real difference, she wondered, between these ordinary women and herself?

> "You look at other women in their close friendships, you look at women on the bus, on the street, in all sorts of different situations and settings and when they look into the eyes of their close friends, they are in love and they just don't know it... I can see in those women's

> everyday close friendships – a love in their eyes, and having that love is not that different from what I feel." (Virginia, 44)

The old feminist slogan would have us believe that 'any woman can be a lesbian'. It appears that there may be some truth in this after all!

And I thought, trouble!
Carol's story

As we have just seen, one of the troublesome questions that crops up for most lesbians is the old nature/nurture one. Unlike heterosexuals, who are not expected to justify their sexual tastes, lesbians have to ask, why am I like this? Are lesbians born or made? Many, looking back over their earlier lives, will point to feelings or incidents that may have seemed trivial at the time but which, in hindsight, now seem to suggest incipient lesbian 'tendencies'.

I have chosen to include Carol's story here in full, because it shows how complicated this issue can be. A cheerful, quietly spoken woman, Carol only started living as a lesbian in her mid-40s. We spoke over the telephone and this was a particularly moving interview. Carol is one of those rare women able to communicate feelings so strongly that you find yourself laughing along with her infectious giggle and silenced by her honest response to emotional pain. She is clearly very happy in her new life, devoted to her girlfriend, and able to look back with a kind of wry amazement at what she had to go through to get to this happy state. It has not been an easy journey. At times, events seem to have conspired to tear her in two, and she makes no attempt to laugh off the pain of such times or to pretend they were anything other than harrowing. Yet, for all that, it is the irrepressible, laughing side of her that comes through in the end.

Looking back, Carol can identify events that perhaps hint at an existing attraction to women from quite a young age. She also experienced moments of uncertainty about her sexuality that she refers to as "hiccups". But her stable, run-of-the-mill marriage seemed to be jogging along contentedly until (quite literally) a strange door opened and propelled her into lesbian life! Then things became about as difficult as they could be. After an unpleasant divorce, and the anguish of living through long years of uncertainty, hoping that her children would be able to accept her and her new partner, things seemed to settle down for Carol. Even then, as you will see, her troubles were not over.

In terms of whether lesbians are born or made, her account of this difficult journey leaves more questions than answers. Was she somehow 'really' a lesbian all along? Or is she looking back at her crushes on teachers and intense friendships – the kinds of experiences that are, after all, very common among women – and reinterpreting them in the light of her later feelings? Read what Carol has to say, and make up your own mind.

*

Calling myself a lesbian means feeling good about myself at the moment, strong. I don't always use it. I know the people who are happy with it. My son is very happy with it, my daughter is very uncomfortable with it. My mother is sort of... So I wouldn't use those words to make them feel uncomfortable. 'Gay', I would use, but I say 'lesbian' and I would see my daughter shrink. 'Gay' is a softer word to other people, so I suppose I would use it to be caring about other people's feelings.

Terms like 'queer' and 'dyke', I think, are a little bit too rough for me. We have younger friends, and they use them, but they make me cringe. I found it difficult to use the word 'lesbian' at the very beginning. 'Gay' was easy, but I just made myself consciously use the word 'lesbian' to make me realise who I was. I knew it was necessary.

I didn't really sort myself out until I was 40. That's when I left my husband. I'd say about 45 was when I started to think more strongly about myself. Forty was the time when I was having problems sorting out who I really was and what I wanted out of my life. I was married, I had two children. It was an easy marriage, so it was a question of – how can I put this? I didn't want to rock the boat, but I knew I wasn't happy in the situation I was in, and I was starting to need more for myself.

I was 18 years married, and five years before that with the person I married, from childhood to marriage. I did go out with other boys, but nothing at all interesting. I met my future husband when I was 15. My husband was the sort of man who was, well, not like my father! My father was the aggressive, ordinary sort of man; macho, Irishman, boss, domineering. My husband was kind, gentle, caring, considerate, easy to get along with, friendly – all the positive things you ever see in a man. So I went towards him becuase he was not like my father, which is probably why the marriage lasted so long, because he stayed like that all the way through and we didn't argue. But, *bland* is the way to describe it; it just drifted into the marriage stakes. I didn't really question it, but you just went along with the way people thought. Yes, I had a few hiccups, I was attracted to women, but I thought it was a phase and I just didn't take it on. I was so young to mature anyway. I was very immature in my sexual needs. I had no needs at all at that stage. I loved him, I cared about him, but I didn't fall in love; no, never.

I didn't fall in love with other boys, either. I was terribly immature. I didn't have those sort of feelings, one way or the other. But when I was 17 I did go to work, and there was a girl – a woman, rather – and I had the feeling I just wanted to be with her, but I didn't know why and I didn't question it at all. My parents never asked me if I was doing the right thing, or if I felt the right thing for my husband. They just assumed because he was so nice, it was going to be a good marriage.

I had a crush on a teacher at school. Then, we all put it down to the usual phase, but it was never discussed, it was just something I kept to myself. You just didn't talk about feelings, no matter what sort of feelings they were. I had a very strong attachment to this teacher, which I didn't discuss at all with anybody. Then, when I was with my husband I worked with this girl and, yes, I couldn't get her out of my mind. But I still stuck with my boyfriend, as it were, because he was very safe. Those feelings were, I think, quite disturbing at the time. I just blocked it off.

When we had been married for about 15 years, we lived in Westlington.

Somebody moved in further down the road, and they were having one of these silly parties and came to invite us to go. And I opened the door and I went *boompf* for no reason at all. I had never met this person before in my life, and as soon as I saw her I thought... trouble!

By then I had been having 'hiccups' for a long time. I was bored. Terribly bored. But boredom is not enough to stop a marriage, especially when it's basically solid. But anything else with my husband was – well, we had our problems. How we conceived children I never know half the time. He was an innocent as I was, and we didn't grow. I mean totally innocent. We were even both virgins when we got married, and yet I had been going with him since I was 15. I didn't get married until I was 22, poor chap! We just said no, but now I know why it was so *easy* to say no!

The woman at the door was straight. But she did string me along. It came out in the end, very strongly, and lots of things happened. To put it in a nutshell, her husband became attracted to me. That was quite funny, really. He made it clear how he felt, and unfortunately he wrote a letter, and my husband picked it up and read it and confronted the guy. And his wife said, it's not you she loves, it's me. So it got a little bit messy at that stage.

It was excruciating. This went on for a couple of years before it got to that point. It made it more difficult with my marriage and more difficult with her, because she was overly friendly, but not friendly enough. It was *really* difficult. She liked the attention and also, I was working, and she enjoyed the little bit of extras spent on her, and we had a good time. Swimming, all the sorts of things you do with ordinary friends, but it just had an extra zizz to it. It did come to a head, and all four of us had a talk about the whole situation, and it was left that I didn't have much to do with her, but I still couldn't drop it, and I rang Gay Switchboard.

That's another complicated story! I had a friend where I worked and she suggested I went to marriage guidance. I did mention it to my husband, but he was not interested, so I went by myself and the friend of mine came with me to encourage me to get there. And I went in, and I couldn't speak for ten minutes. The counsellor was very good, and I just couldn't get it out of my mouth. In the end I said I was in love with someone who wasn't my husband, and I just found it really difficult to say it was a woman. I had a long talk with her and she did ask me – this is really embarrassing, I don't know if I can talk about it – she asked if I had ever reached a climax with my husband. And, in all those years, I hadn't. She was... surprised. Whether it was in her job description or not, she took me along to Anne Summers [the sex shop], would you believe, which opened my eyes a little bit. I was so innocent, you've no idea!

I went back [to marriage guidance] a couple of times, and she suggested I ring the Gay Switchboard, which I did do, although I found it extremely difficult, and I arranged to meet the person who was on the other end. It was – well, I *really* didn't know what to expect, because I had never met a gay person before. I was 39, didn't know what to expect. She was really nice, a compassionate, kind person who actually worked in the next office block to me. So we had lunch and got together, and then we had another meeting, at which she introduced me to her partner, and that was a bit more daunting. And then she took me to the gay pub, which was *really* daunting! I didn't connect with those people at all, because it was a horrible place in those days. I have not been there since. I thought, what am I doing here? I should be at home with my family. The guilt. I felt terrible. It just seemed so wrong, and I didn't identify with any of the people.

Anyway, after a while the lady from Switchboard did suggest having a meeting of people who were interested and introducing people she had spoken to on Switchboard. A meeting was arranged; we didn't know how many people would turn up, but I went. Only two people turned up, and it was me and the woman who is now my partner! We have been together for 15 years. She also had real problems; she had only just discovered she was gay, so they tried to discourage us, saying we had both got too much baggage. Joy had had twelve years of family problems but she didn't realise it was because she was gay. That is how we got together, but then the problems started with my family.

I talked on the phone to a friend from another part of the country. She has been my friend since we were four. She was brilliant, really surprised – nobody dreamed in a million years that I had these lesbian thoughts. Then I did get my husband to meet the people from Gay Switchboard, but it didn't go very well, because he was the sort of chap who thought nothing was ever his fault. Nice though he was, nothing was his fault. Very pompous, he thought it was his world, he had this sort of important job.

Then it came to a head. Joy's brother had a nice flat, and I asked my husband if I could go down there and he said yes, but when I came back he made the ultimatum – obviously he had twigged – so he said, either you stay here or you go. Tonight. So he didn't expect me to say, 'I'm off'; it was very much his attitude, of being in command and not expecting me to turn it all upside down, and I did go. But it was too hard. I couldn't leave the children. My daughter was 15, my son was twelve, and I lived for them. The flat wasn't too far away, only five minutes in the car. I went back home every other evening and I spoke to my daughter every morning before she went to school. I went back every other night to sort out the children's clothes and change their beds. But the guilt was too hard, and I went back.

But I couldn't stay, I couldn't do that. I only went back for one night. My husband was working away that night so I didn't have to be with him; we didn't talk about it. But when he came back the next day, I was just so distressed I couldn't stay. I was too distressed to go and too distressed to stay. It was horrendous. I did leave. The saddest part was my daughter, we were so close. She was one of those young people who listen to the radio all the time, at that age, and she'd sent one of these requests up, to say, Mummy, I'm so pleased you're coming home. I think she's still got the tape. I can't talk about it. It was awful.

My husband went for a divorce and I didn't contest it. Got the divorce. We had joint care and control, so I wasn't going to fight. He's in the law, and no matter what happened he would have won. The children wouldn't have come with me anyway, because they were still on his side at that time. A few months later he moved to the neighbouring county, because he couldn't stand me coming up all the time. But I used to go up there twice a week. He thought he'd got rid of me, but he hadn't. When she was 18 – the day she became 18 – my daughter moved back with us. She said she felt she couldn't until then. But it was difficult. My son wouldn't speak to us for years, but he is now with us for a short time. It has worked out fine eventually. But I wouldn't recommend it to anybody.

My feelings for Joy, that's the whole point. I felt as if I was living under a black cloud, because I was really torn. I knew I had to be with Joy, but I wanted to be with my children. So there was a terrible blackness for years until it sorted itself out, and it did eventually. But it took a lot of struggle. We were determined not to give up on the children, which we could easily have done, and I am sure a lot of people in that situation do. My husband basically helped it along the way, because he was so awful, he was hopeless. It helped me a great deal. Joy was so patient and understanding of my needs, so it worked out eventually.

If I had known all along that I was a lesbian, I don't know which way I would have gone. Purely because I think I always wanted children, it is an easier way, to be straight. I think I would have allowed myself to be myself, but that would have been hard, even so. Because then you have the extra problems later on, of family and children, so in a way I am glad it worked out like it has, because I feel I have actually got the best of both worlds.

Was I born gay? That's a very difficult one. I really don't know. I was brought up in a household that was terribly matriarchal; I could only relate to women. I was talking about this the other night to my son, because he needed questions answered. It was the first time I had ever had a really good talk to him, and he wanted to go from the beginning. I just said I was brought up in a really strong matriarchal society, and then, when a man came in from the outside when I was about three or four, putting his authority on to the home where I lived, I didn't like it. Also, him giving the boy the added advantages, or so I thought at the time. I always preferred the company of women. I think I was attracted to a man once, only once, but mostly women. So I don't know if I was born that way, or whether I was made that way. But I prefer it!

It should be so easy to say what I prefer, but it's not. Apart from the physical things about women, which are *very* high up my list! I can't stand men's bodies; I don't know how I managed to stay married for so long! I am – yeuch – so against men I don't know how I did it. Looking back, in hindsight, I probably always was like this – I just don't like men's bodies. My partner is so... We are tuned in, we think the same. No, that sounds boring doesn't it, we don't think the same! We have the same consideration for each other. We care about people in the same way. I am sure men do, but they think about life on a completely different level. They don't talk on the same levels. I'm sure there are men out there that would but, apart from my son, I haven't met anybody like that. I think it's amazing he's like that! Maybe we haven't given them a chance yet, this new generation of men. Maybe they are more like that, but the older generation certainly are very blocked.

And my sex life is *very* different. Very much so. Woke up, shattered, exploded. And I think you have got to have that, whether you are straight or gay, to sustain any relationship. Sexual passion is important with us, especially now. We are in a terrible state of limbo as Joy has been diagnosed with multiple sclerosis and it is really difficult. She is only 46, so it's really difficult with work and everything. I know it will work between the two of us, and we have got what we need to have from each other mentally as well as physically. We've still got the zizz. But we are both young – ish! We had ten years working together, which was hard graft but we loved it. Although it was very hard and caused a lot of stress... I know it contributed to my illness, and might have contributed to hers as well, I don't know. But now she is doing a job she can maintain, her own business, and hopefully we will continue as long as we can, until maybe we get a cure. Maybe. That's it.

Notes

1. For detailed discussion, see the chapter 'A History of Ideas about Sexuality: Culture and Religion', in Tamsin Wilton, *Sexualities in Health and Social Care: A textbook*, Open University Press, Buckingham, 2000.
2. For more on this research, see the chapter 'Science and Sexuality: The medical model and its implications', Ibid.
3. For a detailed overview, see Edward Stein, *The Mismeasure of Desire: The science, theory and ethics of sexual orientation*, Oxford University Press, Oxford, 1999.
4. Mary McIntosh (1968) 'The Homosexual Role'. The paper was first published in the academic journal *Social Problems*, but has been widely reprinted in lesbian and gay studies anthologies.
5. See, for example, Tamsin Wilton, *Good for You: A handbook on lesbian health and wellbeing*, Cassell, 1997; or Sue O'Sullivan (ed), *Women's Health: A Spare Rib reader*, Pandora, London, 1987.

6

LEARNING FROM EXPERIENCE

> *"I really enjoyed talking to you. I hope your work continues to go well, and that it really does go some way towards changing attitudes for the better. I would love to help in some way, as I remember the biggest thing for me at the time it happened was the feeling of total isolation – of not knowing anyone else in the same situation, and I'm sure if I'd had just one person to say, 'It's okay, you're not on your own, there are lots of other women who've been through the same thing' it would have helped me so much. Instead, I have had to dig away to find my own path, and if I could share the road-map with someone else, I would happily do that." (Letter from one of the women who took part in this project, received after her interview)*

This letter movingly expresses a hope shared by many women who took part in this research – me included – that making these stories public would make a difference. We all felt that some of the lessons that had been learned so painfully by individual women, often in isolation and with little support, could be of use to others making their own transition to a lesbian life. Clearly, there are also lessons to be learnt by the wider lesbian community and even by mainstream society, which so often fails its lesbian members.

This chapter draws out some of those lessons and suggests strategies for changing things for the better. It is followed by a resources section, where you will find suggestions for further reading as well as contact details for sources of support. Of course, nobody can offer easy solutions to complicated real-life problems, and nothing here should be taken as such. Nor are these 'rules' or even 'guidelines' for coming out. They are perhaps best thought of as friendly advice, based on the experiences of 80 women who have all been through the process of questioning and redefining their sexuality. The first section speaks to individual women who, whatever their circumstances, have been touched by some of these issues. The second is for all of us in the wider lesbian community which, whether you believe in it or not, turns out to be such a key element in the lives of women who turn their backs on heterosexuality and look to other lesbians to help them rethink their lives and identities.

Finally, the chapter concludes with a discussion of some of the implications of this research for society more generally. After her interview, one woman said she could "teach Jack Straw a thing or two!" Straw was home secretary at the time, and was doing nothing to advance the cause of lesbian and gay civil rights. Somehow I find it hard to imagine any member of the Cabinet finding the time to peruse these pages but, dear reader, should you indeed happen to be the home secretary, you will find plenty to interest you in the final section of this chapter!

Words of wisdom for the newly hatched lesbian

The first thing to bear in mind, if you are one of those who discovers the joys of lesbian love later in life, is that you are *not* alone. Far from it. Almost all research into lesbian identity (with the exception of studies done in the bad old days, when the only women who co-operated with researchers were those hoping to be cured or in trouble with the law) have found the same thing; *most* lesbians spend at least part of their lives as heterosexuals.[1]

Many explanations for this have been put forward. Some suggest that women have a weaker 'sex drive' than men, so that it takes longer for a woman to recognise her lesbian 'urges'. Others put it down to socialisation, pointing out that it is only in recent years that women have been recognised as sexual beings at all. Still others point to the importance of motherhood. Women are, after all, under a great deal of social pressure to find a mate and have children, and this pressure is powerful enough to override their sexual orientation. The desire for children was certainly something expressed by many of the women in this study, some of whom did, indeed, wonder whether this had delayed their recognition of their attraction to women.

I suspect that many of those trying to find an explanation for this phenomenon are motivated by their own anxiety. Heterosexuality has been granted very high social and cultural status. Moreover, the institutions of the state are all organised around the assumption that most citizens will live heterosexual lives. This is why so many politicians express the fear that homosexuality is capable of destroying the family, the social fabric, even the nation itself! There is a lot invested in heterosexuality, which is why we are all told so often that it is normal, natural, morally right, proper and deeply exciting.

To see women simply reject all this is very threatening to those who want to maintain the status quo. Most of the 'explanations' for previously heterosexual women coming out as lesbians assume that they must actually have been lesbians all along, because only a real lesbian could possibly think that being with another woman was better than being with a man. Because being with a man is the most wonderful thing that can happen to a 'real' woman. Got it?

I am not saying that these explanations are wrong. It may, indeed, be the case that a woman who would be much happier with another woman gets married because of social pressures. We have heard such stories in these pages. We have also seen, however, that a woman can be perfectly content in her heterosexual life and that her sexuality can simply *change*. Only you can say what your experience has been, and there is no valid reason why you should try to make it fit into anyone else's theories. Human sexuality is extremely complex. It is also very tangled up with social rules and regulations, psychological insecurities and cultural norms. We are, frankly, nowhere near being able to claim that we understand it. So none of us should feel under any pressure to explain or justify our sexual preferences and choices in terms of existing categories. What happens, happens.

Nor is there any 'right' way to be a lesbian. The woman who feels very strongly that she was born a lesbian, who has never so much as kissed a man and who has lived as a lesbian all her life is neither more nor less 'real' than the woman who falls in love with her best friend and comes out at the age of 50. It is likely that the life-long lesbian has had to deal with some very difficult situations that the 'new' lesbian has not had to confront. Women who come out at 30, 40 or 50 do not know what it is like trying to survive in the school playground or out on the street as a lesbian teenager. They also have the advantage of being able to give a ready answer to some cocksure man who tells them they're only gay because they haven't met the right man yet, or that they don't know what they're missing.

On the other hand, they may have to deal with problems that most life-long lesbians don't have to face. Ending a marriage is not easy. Divorce is *not* the same thing as ending a lesbian relationship, because the state and the legal profession move in and start poking about in your intimate affairs. Of course, plenty of lesbians have and bring up children with other lesbians, and this can lead to much pain and anguish if the relationship ends. But fighting to be allowed to keep your kids is an altogether different matter when their biological father and his family are trying to take them away from you. If this happens, it can feel as if the whole weight of heterosexual 'normality' is lined up against you.

In short, there is nothing at all to be gained from the sorts of in-fighting that can sometimes go on between those who have come to lesbian life along very different paths. The name 'lesbian' is not some kind of formal qualification. You don't have to sit an exam, you don't have to wear the insignia and nobody has the right to award the title, nor to take it off you if they think you have lied on your CV. The planet is still largely inhabited by people who think we should be exterminated or locked up. That being so, any woman who calls herself 'lesbian', 'gay woman' or 'dyke' must have very good reasons for doing so and her choice of name must be respected.

OK, so no, you are not alone and, yes, you do have every right to call yourself a lesbian. But there is more to changing your sexual identity than plucking up the courage to think of yourself as gay. You have to tell other people, you have to come out of the closet, even if you didn't know you were in it in the first place. And this is not something that you do once, sigh with relief and never have to do again. You will have to decide whether or not to come out, who to, when, where and how, for as long as you live as a lesbian.

Imagine you find yourself having to move house and wondering whether the removal men will treat your possessions with a little less care if they realise that you are gay. Should you pack up all the 'lesbian stuff' yourself and have it safely in boxes before they turn up? If you come out to your refuse collectors, will they handle your rubbish more carelessly? If you don't, are you pretending to be straight and letting down the lesbian nation? Should you come out to your dentist? If so, is it a good idea to do so when your mouth is full of steel or to wait until you have had a good rinse and spit? Is it fair on your hamster if you come out to the vet during a tricky internal examination? These questions never stop. I still don't know if my milkman knows...

Importantly, nobody has the right to tell you how, when or where to come out, nor who you should tell and why. You lover may be out to her entire family, her workmates and viewers of her television programme, but she is in no position to know what the response of *your* friends and family will be.

It is perfectly true that being 'out' is a lot easier to deal with than being closeted. Studies have shown that individuals who are open and confident about their sexuality are generally happier and less prone to stress and depression. But you can interpret such findings in two ways. Yes, it may be the case that being out contributes to psychological wellbeing. Indeed, this is likely to be so, since the closet is a stressful place to get stuck. But it may also be that having tolerant parents, or friends who love and accept you for yourself, gives you the confidence to come out in a relaxed way. After all, wouldn't you be confident if you had grown up with loving, open-minded parents?

Coming out to parents

We have seen throughout this book that life is a lot easier when your parents are able to accept and support you, and that they can cause their own brand of havoc if they are not. Based on this evidence, think carefully about how to come out to your own parents. How do you think they will react? Bear in mind that, even if they react badly, they may well become more accepting in time. If you anticipate that your mum will be more understanding than your dad, or vice versa, consider telling the 'easier' parent first and enlisting their help in breaking the news to the more 'difficult' one. Remember that this has worked for some women.

Don't forget that this is difficult information for parents to take in. There is almost no accurate and unbiased information about lesbians circulating in mainstream culture. You may have discovered this when trying to find things out for yourself! You will have to be the 'adult' now, in relation to your parents. You may have to be patient, explaining things to them, helping them to recognise old stereotypes and reject unhelpful myths.

Educating bigoted or ill-informed parents can be very painful. Nobody likes to sit and listen to offensive garbage about their deepest feelings, especially when it comes out of the mouth of their mum or dad. But you do have an important advantage. You have a certain amount of control over when and how you tell them, and you have access to information they don't have. So, plan it carefully and get as much support as you can. Start with the resources section at the back of this book. Get hold of one of the books that are listed there. Get in touch with a group like Families and Friends of Lesbians And Gays (FFLAG), or Stonewall, and ask them to send you information leaflets you can give to your parents. Ring up the London Lesbian and Gay Switchboard (or get the number for your local lesbian line or switchboard from the phonebook or the gay press) and ask for advice and backup. If your parents' religious beliefs are a stumbling block, get in touch with one of the lesbian and gay religious organisations.

Women who come out later on in life are less likely to be dependent on their parents for accommodation and support. They are therefore unlikely to find themselves thrown out on to the streets with no source of income, as happens all too often to younger lesbians. If you are, for whatever reason, financially dependent on your parents, think very carefully before you come out to them. If you think there is any likelihood of them withdrawing their support, there is little point in telling them the truth. Remember Michelle, who knew her parents' religious beliefs meant "they would certainly throw me out of the family" and who therefore decided to wait until she had got the professional qualifications she was studying for and could leave home. You may feel uneasy about taking your parents' money under 'false pretences', but it is not your sexuality that is unethical, it is their prejudice. You have every right to protect yourself against the consequences of bigotry.

Even when your material wellbeing is not at stake, the prospect of parental rejection can stir up childhood memories and feel very frightening in consequence. Yet a daughter planning to tell a parent the truth about her sexuality is, in many ways, the stronger of the two. Remember that your parents may be frightened for you. Think about how you can reassure them that you are not going to have a miserable life, that you are happy and that this is a positive change. Perhaps show them one of the stories in this book. They may, if they have picked up some of the old psychological explanations of homosexuality, feel that it must be their 'fault', that something about the way you were brought up has caused your lesbianism. Such beliefs may cause guilt, which may, in turn, be expressed in anger and hostility. You don't have to give them a scholarly lecture on theories of sexual orientation at this point! Simply repeat that you are happy, that if you thought they *were* responsible you would be very grateful but that these theories have been pretty much disproved. Offer to help them find out more if they need to, or suggest that they ring the Lesbian and Gay Switchboard.

Remember, too, that you have enough to do living your own life. Although you can help your parents come to terms with the 'new' you, it is not your job to take care of them and make everything all right for them. They are adults, and perfectly capable of finding things out for themselves if you point them in the right direction. Don't allow yourself to be made to feel guilty, either. You have not done anything wrong, and a lesbian is not a bad thing to be. Something that emerges very clearly in the stories in this book is that a lesbian life can be immensely fulfilling and nourishing for women. You have the right to find happiness in your own way, and you do not have to abide by your parents' rules for living. And, if your parents are quite cheerful about the whole thing, or claim in an amused and tolerant way that they suspected something ever since you rejected your dollies in infancy, thank your lucky stars and give them a hug from me!

Coming out to friends

There are crucial differences between parents and friends when it comes to telling them about your new sexual identity. Parents have their roots deep in our psyche, in a way that friends just don't. Our friends are also people we have chosen to be close too, unlike our parents who decided to be part of our lives before we were even born! For both these reasons, coming out to friends is less of a big deal and probably less likely to result in emotional upheaval. It is not, however, always possible to predict how friends will respond to your news.

We tend to have friends who hold similar views to our own, and who share our belief system. This means that, if you have lived a fairly conventional heterosexual life, your friends may have fairly conventional views on homosexuality and be unable to offer informed support when you come out to them. The issue of sexuality, however, may be a surprisingly difficult one for even the most broadminded liberal when it concerns a close friend.

The problem here may be a moral one, or expressed as such, but it is perhaps more likely to be psychological. Heterosexual women friends may feel rejected or judged by your decision to ditch men. You have, after all, rejected something which is a central (if unchallenged) feature of their own lives. Friends who are less than satisfied with their own lives may feel envious of your ability to make such a positive change, and those with uninspiring sex lives may feel jealous of what they imagine to be your decadent hours of pleasure.

Another gremlin which tends to pop up when new lesbians come out to their straight women friends is to do with the unspoken level of sexual attraction which underpins many close friendships between heterosexual women. Your announcement may pull the covers off these unrecognised feelings, leaving your straight friend to deal with some unusual emotions. She may feel sexually rejected ("Why has she fallen in love with another woman? She should be in love with me!") or may find herself having to acknowledge her own attraction to you. These are not easy things to deal with, as you know. Some lesbians report that their straight friends make a pass at them (a long time chum of mine suddenly confessed to harbouring erotic fantasies about me for years), which at least means that they are able to acknowledge something, however uncomfortable you may feel with their method of expressing it!

On the other hand, women who cannot cope when subterranean desires are thrown into the spotlight may simply shut down their affectionate feelings towards you altogether. It can be extremely painful when a newly out lesbian finds herself completely rejected by a woman friend. If this happens to you, the reason may be not that she doesn't like you any more, but that she is scared she may like you too much. For this reason, it is often the closest and most intimate friendships that collapse and vanish without trace. I lost two female best friends when I came out. One used to call me 'best-beloved' and we were so affectionate with each other that my boyfriend was convinced we secretly fancied each other. The other was accustomed to spending quality time with me on a twice-weekly basis, usually moaning about the sexual inadequacies of men. At the time I found their defection hurtful and confusing but, with the benefit of hindsight, it started to make sense.

Luckily, the evidence here seems to suggest that most friends are accepting and enormously supportive. Several women in this study stressed that their existing friendship network had been *more* supportive than lesbians they knew. Given enough time to get used to the idea, even friends who react negatively tend to come around in the end. If you want to keep a friendship going with someone who finds your sexuality difficult, it may be worthwhile educating them using the method suggested above for parents. Lend them a book to read, or get them to ring one of the numbers in the resources section. If they refuse to co-operate, back off. You don't have time or energy to spare, and if they are not taking any steps towards you, chances are you are not going to make much difference. Be reassured that, even now, they may well come around in the end.

Some friends, however, never come around. For whatever reason, certain individuals seem to be unable to come to terms with people they are close to changing their sexuality. The two women friends who reacted badly when I came out to them have simply taken themselves out of my life. I bump into one of them from time to time and we make polite conversation, but I haven't seen or heard from the other for 14 years. Several women who took part in this study mentioned that they had lost friends, or that the group they used to hang out with didn't seem to want to know them any longer. Others stressed that it was less close friends who had reacted badly; other mothers who used to chat at the school gate, or casual acquaintances in the neighbourhood who no longer smiled at them in the street. To some extent, coming out to friends and acquaintances can be thought of as a litmus test – how valuable a friendship was it anyway, if it can be destroyed by this information? It isn't always this simple, however, and there is no doubt that being dropped by a friend you come out to can be a true loss and cause you real pain.

For women who leave husbands or male partners to live a lesbian life, there is a further complication. What happens to all those friends you shared as a heterosexual couple? This is, of course, a problem for everyone who goes through a relationship breakup, with one partner or the other getting 'custody' of particular friends. For the new lesbian, there may be additional discomfort in seeing friends take the side of her ex. It is all too easy to feel that he ends up with all the friends because of homophobia, or (and here guilt kicks in), because she has behaved really wickedly in leaving this nice man and breaking up the family to satisfy her own perverted lusts. Calm down! Leaving an unhappy relationship for a new life is something people do all the time. There is nothing about the fact that your new life is a lesbian one that makes what you are doing any worse than usual. Relationship breakups are always messy, and divorces are famously agonising. Your being a lesbian doesn't change that.

It helps if you can gain enough detachment to feel sorry for your ex. He, after all, is left in the heterosexual life you have left behind. While you go off, exploring your new self, forging new and exciting relationships and widening the boundaries of human experience, he is stuck in Normsville. Perhaps he could use a little extra support from the heterosexual friends whose lifestyle you are also rejecting? It may be best just to let them get on with it.

If it is any consolation, the lesbian world is not much better when it comes to taking sides when long-term relationships end. In fact, because gay people have so much invested in the success of long-term gay relationships, things can be even worse. I have lost count of the times I have heard (or have uttered myself) the anguished cry "Petronella and Cindy *cannot* split up! They are the longest-lasting lesbian couple in the entire *city*! We *need* them to be together!" The friendship 'custody battle' that takes place when heterosexual relationships end is confined to a friendship group; it doesn't affect the entire heterosexual community. For lesbians, the friendship group often *is* the entire local lesbian community. And there is nothing on earth quite like a close-knit lesbian community that finds itself split into two hostile camps over whether Cindy or Petronella is the injured party. Welcome to the cutting edge of human sexuality!

Coming out to your boss

Lesbians in Britain currently have more legal protection than at any time in the nation's history. Sadly, when it comes to employment legislation, this isn't saying much. Put simply, if your boss wants to get rid of you, it is more than likely that she or he can. Of course some jobs are more protected than others, and most people have a pretty fair idea about how vulnerable they are to the possibility of dismissal. Nevertheless, hanging on in a job where the boss wants you out is far from easy, and in any case not good for one's mental wellbeing. Nor is it easy to sue for wrongful dismissal, to haul your employer before an industrial tribunal or to fight a lengthy legal battle to persuade the courts that subsection ii(p) of clause 18 of paragraph 174 of an obscure piece of legislation applies to your particular case. The lesbian and gay world depends on the bravery of those individuals who *do* take their cases through the courts, but nobody says you have to become a figurehead of your community before you have got used to being gay yet. So, think *very* carefully before coming out at work.

Again, the workplace is well-known for producing particular stresses for those who conceal their sexuality. Having to watch what you say when sharing details about your holiday or weekend activities is draining, as is rounding up a docile person of the male persuasion to be your 'boyfriend' at the firm's annual dinner-dance. So there is much to be said for not having to put yourself through all this. There is, however, much to be said for being in a job, particularly if you have children to feed.

The ideal is to be fully open and confident about your sexuality in a workplace where nobody minds and where the board of directors is crammed with openly gay people and a handful of broad-minded heterosexuals. The next best is to find yourself in a workplace – much like my own university – where there are plenty of other confidently 'out' gay people, most of your heterosexual colleagues generally succeed in coping with their feelings of discomfort and a dwindling number of bigots have to content themselves with stirring up what trouble they can behind your back. Most of us have to put up with something along these lines.

In the first flush of joy in your new life it may be tempting to come out to *everyone*. If there is any possibility that this could make life difficult for you at work, stop, think, and plan carefully. Check out your contract, talk with your union. If you aren't in a union, it is worth thinking about joining one now, even if your workplace isn't unionised. Most of the major unions now have policies in support of their lesbian and gay members. You may find that local union reps are not well-informed about these issues, in which case get in touch with the national office. Then, plan a careful coming-out strategy, trying to arrange it so that you can find some support within your place of work before you come out to management. Of course, there is little point coming out to management if they are located miles away and don't know who you are, though it might still be a good idea quietly to check company policy on sexual orientation, just so you know where you stand.

Most workplaces nowadays seem fairly unconcerned about the sexuality of their employees. If you work with children, however, you may meet some misunderstanding. Teachers in state schools have the support of the teaching unions, all of whom have policies in place to protect their lesbian and gay staff. Social workers are also protected by their professional body, as are many others who work for local authorities. However, those who work in public schools, private nurseries or other non-statutory bodies may find they are less well protected. In addition, all the supportive policies in the world cannot help if headteachers, directors of social services or other managers refuse to implement them. In case of trouble, make use of the resources section to find appropriate advice.

This section has, of necessity, been a little alarming. So it is important to remind you that employment issues did *not* emerge as a major problem for the women who took part in this study. Nobody got fired, nobody had to face a hostile boss, nobody thought they had been actively discriminated against. One woman, you will recall, did say that a prospective employer had turned against her when informed by a third party that she was a lesbian, and several women reported that they made a decision *not* to be out at work. Given the size of the sample, this doesn't suggest that workplace problems are inevitable, rather the opposite.

Coming out to your kids

One thing that emerges very clearly from listening to the mothers who took part in this study is that making the transition to a lesbian life makes particularly difficult demands on women with children. The nature of these demands also shifts, depending on the ages of the children involved. Women whose children were younger experienced fewer problems than mothers of teenagers, although they also clearly worried about the possibility that adolescence would bring additional problems with it.

From their evidence it seems to be the case that younger children don't really care if Mummy's partner is another woman, provided that their own needs continue to be met. These needs are the same as those of any other child going through family breakup; to be reassured that both parents still love them, to be able to spend time with both parents, to have a settled home, to have as much 'normality' as possible in daily life and to have the loving ear of a sympathetic parent. Depending on the age of the child, they may be helped to feel secure in the midst of family upheaval by such things as extra cuddles, the continued presence of favourite toys and/or pets, unbroken rituals for bedtime/meals/visits to grandparents etc., continuing contact with their friends and with members of the extended family, extra support at playgroup, nursery or school and being told as much as seems appropriate about what is going on.

This is true in all circumstances. Lesbian mothers may, however, have additional things to deal with. Grandparents may, as we have seen, refuse to accept that a lesbian is the right person to bring up their grandchildren, and this can be very destructive. It is important that parents who separate do *not* allow themselves to say damaging things about the other parent in the hearing of their young children, and this can be particularly dificult for fathers when the end of the marriage is connected in some way to their wife coming out as a lesbian.

It is very important to know that, despite all the social and psychological difficulties involved, many men are capable of being remarkably responsible and supportive in such circumstances. Simply knowing that this is the case may help to persuade a man who is behaving selfishly that this is not the only way to do it. If you find yourself in the unlucky position of having to manage a male partner and/or parents or in-laws who are making life difficult for you and your children, don't put up with it. Get advice from an agency like Relate (formerly Marriage Guidance), who are increasingly equipped to deal with lesbian and gay clients and who may be able to offer mediation to enable you all to resolve things in the best interests of your child(ren). Get in touch with other lesbian mums (there are lots of us, and there are bound to be some within reach of your area) and get moral and practical support from others who have been there too. If push comes to shove, find a solicitor who is sympathetic to, and has some experience of, situations like yours. Gay-friendly solicitors are increasingly easy to find. They advertise in the gay press (try *Diva, Gay Times* or the *Pink Paper*); or get local details from a helpline. Pink Parents (see resources section) should also be able to offer support, advice and information.

Sorting out the practicalities and dealing with other adults is one thing, explaining the situation to your children is another. Here, trust your instincts. You know your own child better than anyone, and you probably have a pretty good idea about what information they can cope with. Younger children are likely to be perfectly happy with the information that Mummy loves her new friend Jill very much indeed, they don't necessarily need to have the relationship labelled 'lesbian', and won't have a context for thinking about anything to do with sex. Some, however, will need to check out with you information or name-calling they may have met in the playground. If your seven-year-old asks "Mummy, is it true that you are a lezzie?", you will have to use your judgement about how to respond. Remember that children love their parents unquestioningly, and want to carry on doing so. What is needed from you is honest, straightforward information delivered without fuss or anxiety.

It can also help to defuse anxiety if you create playful ways of incorporating the issue into your family culture. I know of a least one lesbian household where the epithet 'son-of-a-gun' has been replaced by 'son-of-a-dyke' as a term of affection for the lively youngest boy. Not every mother would feel comfortable with this, but it certainly reassured all the children in the family that there was nothing shameful about their mothers' lives.

Older children pose different problems. An image-conscious 16-year-old is not going to be placated by nursery rhymes. Stress can reveal just how young and vulnerable teenagers still are and how they (and you) react to this depends on who you all are and how you deal with each other. Children of all ages may 'regress' during times of insecurity. Younger children may wet the bed or return to thumb-sucking. For older children, experiencing strong feelings of grief, insecurity or fear may feel shameful. They may feel that such emotions are childish and to be grown out of. It helps to know that adults feel them too and, if you are lucky, you may get a chance to explain this to them. But teenagers are famously difficult to predict. It is all part of turning into a distinct person. So you may find yourself struggling to get your arms around your six-foot-tall rugby-playing son as he sobs on your shoulder or, on the other hand, straining to hear any sound at all from the bedroom where your furious daughter has locked herself away from all human contact for weeks.

The evidence here from lesbian mothers of teenagers is, be patient. They generally seem to sort things out in their own minds, and most lesbian mothers end up on good terms with their young adult children. For some this takes a long time. It can be profoundly distressing to wait months, or even years, in the hopes that a furious child will eventually accept you and allow you into their life again. Again, remember that this happens to lots of people, not only lesbian mothers.

Finding the lesbian community

As we have seen, the most visible aspect of the lesbian community may have little to offer to lesbians who come out later in life. In particular the 'scene', of clubs, discos, bars and pubs, is dominated by (a) gay men and (b) young people. A 30-year-old mother of two, happily settled with her new lesbian partner and trying to juggle work and childcare, does not necessarily want to spend all her leisure time dancing to ear-splitting music in some smoky club. Risking the perils of passive smoking and hearing loss or succumbing to style-slavery are generally the pastimes of choice of the young.

However, there is more to lesbian life than the scene. Much more. There are small, localised lesbian communities (see below), but there is also a vast network of lesbian activity that covers every corner of the British Isles (yes, even your bit!) and, indeed, reaches around the planet. Several women here explained how important this wider lesbian community had been to them. Gay magazines, television programmes or community radio stations had been lifelines. Contact ads had helped them find partners or explore their sexuality. Academic courses had given them the self-confidence to come out, or the language with which to understand their feelings for women.

This lesbian community is not populated by stereotypes. It isn't owned by lesbians with particular politics or a certain kind of life story, and it isn't dominated by any ideology. Like any other human enterprise in this white-dominated world, it has its share of racists and it doesn't always serve lesbians from minority ethnic communities as well as it should, but nor is it a whites-only club. Disabled lesbians are increasingly vocal and the lesbian community is, I suspect, marginally better than wider 'able-bodied'[2] society at listening.

The new lesbian can get much-needed support, information and advice from the lesbian community. She can also find out much more about what it means to be a lesbian, and something about the history of lesbian life – an important element in consolidating a lesbian identity. The internet is a good place to start. If you are not online at home then hunt out your nearest cybercafé or a library with free internet access. Remember that all UK university libraries must, by law, allow open public access to their facilities. Although they do *not* have to allow you to borrow books (and they won't, since they generally don't have adequate funds to buy enough for their own students), you should be able to browse and to read books *in situ*. Your local public library should have a good collection of lesbian books – if it doesn't, get it to order some – and a quick trip to your local community bookshop or the nearest branch of Waterstone's should also produce results. Then there is the gay press – invaluable for information about gay-friendly services and full of information about groups in your area. If there is no group in your area, why not start one? A quick two-line contact ad in *Diva* should do the trick.

Lessons for the lesbian community

Here, I am speaking to all the local lesbian 'communities' who manage to survive, against all the odds, in the unwelcoming environs of small towns, rural outposts or medium-sized but boring cities (naming no names). I have been hearing stories about you. Yes, you know who you are. They have not been pleasant stories. What's all this about you telling women they can't be lesbians?

Seriously, there are reasons why some small lesbian communiwties are suspicious of outsiders and newcomers. Delicately balanced interpersonal dynamics can be thrown into chaos by the arrival of someone who doesn't know the history of what's been going on. There are also understandable reasons why some lesbians are wary of bisexual women. In theory, there might be no difference between being dumped for another woman and being dumped for a man, but in practice, there is all the difference in the world. It may also be understandable that a woman who has had to fight since she was ten for the right to live her life as a lesbian should resent someone who has lived a life of happy heterosexual privilege for years and now wants to join the gang.

But we have to ask, what kind of lesbian community do we want? Indeed, what do we want the word 'lesbian' to mean? If there is a correct way to be a lesbian, if there are 'real' lesbians and 'fake' lesbians, who has the right to say what the criteria are? After all, if we are going to organise our communities along those lines, allowing 'real' lesbians in and keeping counterfeit lesbians out, the people who decide the criteria are going to have a lot of power in those communities. So who should those powerful people be?

Perhaps they should be women who are themselves 'real' lesbians. Lesbians who have never had sex with a man, perhaps? But, if that is the case, whole communities are going to be run according to the life experiences of a tiny number of women. Because, for whatever reason, the vast majority of lesbians have had sex with at least one man. Or perhaps lesbians who 'always knew' they were lesbians count as 'real'. In which case, what about those women whose lives didn't offer them the chance to recognise their sexuality? We have heard a lot of their stories here.

Perhaps we should allow the 'experts' to take the lead. After all, the definitions of 'real' lesbian identity that we are using here have come from those experts. Who are they? Well, they are almost all men, almost all heterosexual (although a handful of more recent experts are gay men) and almost all American. Good people to be in charge of lesbian communities? Since women who take so seriously the division into 'real' lesbians and everyone else tend not to like men very much, why are they promulgating the ideas and beliefs of men as the basis for their communities?

I hope my point is made. It is not helpful for local lesbian communities to cling on to man-made myths (such as the one that says lesbians have to be masculine in some way) that were made up in the first place by heterosexual men who wanted to keep us in our place. Nor should we perpetuate the notion that there is a right way of being a lesbian. Of course, this is not at all the same as saying that there is no right way to behave once you are a lesbian. There is, and new lesbians have to learn this implicit etiquette as part of the process of coming out.

One of the joys of being a lesbian is that it sets you free from the curse of femininity. No longer doomed to live according to the expectations of the male-dominated mainstream of our cultures, we are free to explore different aspects of our personalities. This – and not some freak of biology – is why significant numbers of lesbians look and behave in 'masculine' ways. Similarly, as we have heard in this book, there are women who, once they escape from heterosexuality, no longer feel the need to compete with men all the time. Whereas their heterosexual selves felt driven to prove their competence at traditional masculine tasks, their lesbian selves are free to enjoy being as girlie as they wish.

This is what makes the lesbian community so radical, and so terrifying to the heterosexual mainstream. It is a place where women can escape from the shackles of gender socialisation and can allow all aspects of their personalities to flourish in a more psychologically integrated manner. We can play with gender roles, exaggerate them, send them up, enjoy them. But if we start to police them, we destroy our own power and our own radicalism.

Some lesbians seem to feel that the community is under threat from women who, having experienced heterosexual life, reject it. Er... Is it just me, or is this seriously silly? Indeed, I cannot think of a better advertisement for lesbianism. Ex-heterosexual women are living lives that say, "Yes, I have experienced all the wonders that heterosexuality has to offer and, frankly, being gay is much nicer, thank you." This is a fairly powerful message!

These are important points. Any marginalised community, if it is to survive and not stagnate, needs to grow. Not only in terms of numbers, it also needs to grow in terms of development. It needs to be able to include new people and take on their ideas, to revisit traditional practices and beliefs and allow them to evolve. Any local lesbian community that persists in treating new lesbians with suspicion and hostility is signing its own death warrant.

Here I want to stress that, although a significant number of women reported unhelpful responses from their local lesbian community, others were luckier. Many expressed gratitude to the other lesbians they had met, who had welcomed them into their new lives and offered real friendship and support. Others had simply not been able to track down any lesbians at all.

To a certain extent, the non-existence of lesbians is an inevitable part of coming out. I remember it well. Over a period of about six months I went from thinking I lived in a lesbian-free zone to realising that, in fact, the city was positively alive with dykes. This is partly because the process of coming out involves getting rid of your heterosexual blinkers and learning how to operate your 'gaydar', that mysterious sixth sense that enables you to home in on another lesbian at fifty paces in a crowded room. It was also because my new peer-group of experienced lesbians was introducing me to the varied range of lesbian social activity.

This, too, holds a lesson for lesbian communities. All over your area, right now, are women trying as hard as they can to come out. But they can't do it without you. The name of the game here has to be outreach. If you have a lesbian discussion group, reading circle, film club, baby-sitting circle, walking group or whatever, advertise the fact to women in your area. I know, it's nice just the way it is; everybody has already slept with everybody else so there's no high drama. But your group – or, at least, being able to get in touch with at least one of its members – might be a lifeline for a newly hatched lesbian.

It is also important that all of us keep supporting what we have. Grumble about it by all means – how long the phone is engaged at Switchboard, how thin this month's *Diva* was, how fed up you are with all the 'boy stuff' in the *Pink Paper* – but these struggling institutions are essential. Women have come out as a result of a contact ad, they have been able to stay out with support from Switchboard. Unless you think women are better off staying with men, our community needs you.

Lessons for society at large

The first lesson for society generally that emerges from these interviews is about the nature of women's sexuality. Whatever you believe about the nature of desire, it is quite clear that it is neither fixed nor easily explained. We have to be very careful about what language we use to describe our desire from this point on.

The phrase 'sexual orientation' describes desire as fixed and permanent. Individuals are *oriented* towards (that is, turned in the direction of) either men or women (apart, that is, from those who are *bisexually* oriented). It is not a useful term, since it cannot apply to the range of experiences we have witnessed in these pages. I suggest we abandon it. On the other hand, the term 'sexual preference' seems to its critics to suggest a cheerfully casual approach to sexuality. A simple preference, akin to liking red wine more than white, perhaps, does not seem powerful enough to account for a desire that is strong enough to drive people to defy convention, end marriages and risk stigma. Although a preference can be strong – think of vegetarianism as a preference and you understand what I mean here – the phrase carries unhelpful suggestions that desire is a matter of taste. I suggest that we reject this term, too.

This leaves two terms, 'sexuality' and 'sexual identity', both of which are useful. Sexuality is broad, encompassing many things besides the sex of one's partners. It is perhaps best thought of as an aspect of personality and, as such, is as varied as individuals themselves. Claiming that one's sexuality is 'lesbian' does not imply anything about the past (or, indeed, the future). It is merely a description of the present. Sexual identity means something different yet again. Most people would agree that identity is something we construct for ourselves throughout our lives. It has to do with our sense of self, of who we are at a fundamental level, as well as the self that we present to the world. This makes it very useful for lesbians, as it enables us to talk about a whole range of experiences. A woman may recognise or come to terms with her lesbian identity, but she may also build it, explore it, strengthen it, consolidate it or express it. She may also allow the lesbian *aspect* of her identity to come to the fore, whether or not she believes that it has always been a part of her.

Nor do the words that have been used to describe sexual identity since the nineteenth century – homosexual and heterosexual – do a particularly good job when applied to the disparate accounts we have read here. The idea which they express, that individuals are either the homosexual kind of person or the heterosexual kind, cannot be supported by this evidence. You cannot make them work even if you resort to the time-honoured trick of describing these women as bisexual, thus creating a special category to contain those who don't fit the boxes and thus allow the homo/hetero barrier to remain intact.

Playing the trump card of "Oh, they must all be bisexual" is, in fact, self-defeating. The two categories of homosexual and heterosexual can only exist if you create bisexuality as a third category to mop up those left over. And the biological theories can only make sense if those two categories are 'real'. Yet the existence of bisexuality strongly suggests that there can be no biological basis for desire at all. In order for any of the existing biological theories to be correct, bisexuals should not exist. After all, it is rather unlikely that any individual should receive the right blend of hormones, or have a portion of brain tissue that was enlarged to just the right degree, or have half the 'gay gene' or a 50:50 mix of 'gay' and 'straight' genes to cause them to desire both women and men.

So, the scientific theories are inadequate and should be jettisoned. They have never been adequate. They are all based on dubious experimental evidence and none of them has been successfully proved, despite all the time, energy and money invested. The question as to why anyone should have taken them seriously in the first place is an interesting one. Certainly, from the evidence of these interviews, many individuals find a biological explanation useful or comforting, because it helps make sense of events and experiences that they have found disruptive or painful. But why should an entire society need such explanations?

Again, there is a clue in these interviews. If women were *not* led to believe that lesbians were born 'like that', if we grew up believing that it was up to us who we fell in love with, desired, had sex with and made our lives with, the institution of heterosexuality and the men who largely benefit from it might collapse. Lesbian sexual activity is the safest kind there is. Two women making love are at less risk of transmitting disease to one another than any other kind of couple. They don't need contraception, either – and all forms of contraception, except vasectomy, have unpleasant side-effects for women. Unless women are somehow *taught* to respond to each other with disgust, fear or simple disinterest (and this is what many feminists mean by the term 'compulsory heterosexuality'), why would any of us bother to take the risk of having sex with men?

At this point in the history of European culture, there is another issue at stake here. You will recall that many of the women who participated in this project described their female partners as being more highly skilled in the emotional side of love relationships than they had found men to be. Women are socialised from an early age to develop skills in communication (particularly listening attentively!), encouraging trust, building intimacy and demonstrating care and concern for others. Men, on the whole, are not.

This may well be in the process of change, as concerned parents (fathers as well as mothers) strive to bring up emotionally skilled boy children. Such change is slow, however, and not supported by policy makers, taught in schools or recognised by politicians. It will be a long time before a woman in search of an emotionally open, expressive and loving relationship is able to find this as easily with men as she could with women.

There appears to be a growing consensus that the package of behaviours and values that we call 'masculinity' may be damaging to the wellbeing of both women and men. Nor is it any longer of much use to the state. Traditional 'manly' characteristics such as aggression, competitiveness, emotional repression and ambition may have been useful in hand-to-hand combat and industrial capitalism, the activities which laid the foundations for the British Empire. They are not, however, much good in the more complex workplace of the new global economy. There is, it is generally agreed, a crisis in masculinity, and the fallout from this can be spotted throughout the stories that make up this book. Women leave men because they find relationships with women are better for them. This is both a symptom of the 'crisis in masculinity' and likely to contribute to it!

Moreover, social change means that women, at least in economically privileged nations such as Britain and the US, have more economic independence than they have experienced at any other time in recorded history. From this economic freedom flows greater personal autonomy. This large-scale social shift is mirrored in the accounts we have heard here. Women are now able to leave unhappy marriages without fear of destitution and even to set up households entirely independent of men, either alone or with a woman partner. Such autonomy enables women to consider their *own* needs in a way that is simply not possible for women in more restricted societies and has only recently become possible in the West.

The women whose stories we have heard do not all believe that they had much choice over the direction of their sexual desires. Nevertheless, they *have* chosen various ways of integrating those desires into their lives. For some of them, chiefly the younger women who take their autonomy so much for granted, men have not played a hugely significant role. The majority, however, have had significant experience of living in intimate relationships with men. With few exceptions, they have found intimacy with other women gives them much more of what they need. Given the larger social picture outlined above, this should not surprise us.

The simple fact seems to be that, for many women, moving away from heterosexual 'normality' into a lesbian life and identity is extraordinarily positive. It is life-enhancing, self-caring and promotes their wellbeing. And this is so *despite* the often deeply distressing negative consequences that may also be experienced. Romeo and Juliet found that the intoxication of their love for one another made their family feud pale into insignificance. In a similar vein, the experiences of these 'new' lesbians suggest that family disapproval, loss of friends, emotional upheaval and societal homophobia are far less significant than the benefits of lesbian life. The price is, as we have seen, often high, but these women clearly feel that the rewards are well worth it.

Lessons for religious leaders

To be loved, cherished, sexually fulfilled, emotionally nourished, listened to with attention and spoken to with respect are things most human beings would say they want in their love relationships. Many of these women have found that other women are much better than men at providing these things. At this point we need to ask, what on earth is wrong with this? What possible justification can there be for declaring that these relationships are less good, sane, healthy, ethical or valuable than traditional marriages?

This is a question that the churches, in particular, have an obligation to answer. As we have seen, religion plays a largely negative role in the lives of women of faith who want to live as lesbians. Women have described how painful it can be trying to make sense of experiences that they are unable to find any harm in, in the light of the unforgiving and bigoted doctrine of the faith they want to live their life by. Many, though not all, have given up their faith in consequence.

It is not enough for clerics to fall back on taken-for-granted claims about the 'word of god'. There are disagreements and disputations about the interpretation of sacred texts in every religion. Islam, Judaism and Christianity, for example, are all riven with argument about the meaning of references to 'homosexuality' in their sacred texts. This is not surprising. Apart from any other considerations, the Koran, the Bible and the Torah were all written centuries before the concept of homosexuality was coined. Despite the pronouncements of

Christian fundamentalists, for example, the theological argument that homosexuality is against the will of god is extremely weak. There are, on the other hand, powerful and repeated condemnations of usury – yet the whole of the capitalist system is based on usury. If scientists have to ask themselves why so much bad science has gone into half-baked experiments to determine what 'causes' homosexuality, so too must religious leaders ask why they continue to demonise lesbian and gay people on such flimsy theological pretexts.

Lessons for public services

The final key theme that emerged as so significant in these interviews is the failure of public services to meet the reasonable needs of lesbian citizens. This is unjust. Lesbians contribute fully to the public purse; we pay taxes, local authority charges, VAT and national insurance at the same rates as non-lesbians. Yet our schools, in particular, fail us, whether as students, as teachers or as the mothers of students. Far too many women spoke of their fears that their children would be bullied at school for having a lesbian mother. This is inexcusable. Some would say that it is time to repeal Section 28 (of the 1988 Local Government Act), which I would agree with. However, I repeat, Section 28 *does not apply to schools*. There is *no* existing legislation to prevent schools providing adequate support to pupils who are lesbian or gay, or who have lesbian or gay parents.

As I write this, the political climate in Britain seems to be taking further steps towards equality for lesbian and gay citizens. There are legislative moves afoot to provide us with pension and inheritance rights and to offer some kind of formal recognition of our partnerships. Even the Conservative Party, traditionally the home of rabid homophobia, has announced that it would support limited rights for gay couples. Women who step out of the safety of heterosexual life often do not realise just how many privileges and benefits they are giving up. Hopefully, this situation will continue to improve. There are, however, good reasons to suspect that schools – vulnerable as they are to media intrusion – may lag behind wider society in reflecting and promoting this increased tolerance and acceptance. Let's hope that the growing number of lesbian mothers confident enough to be open in their dealings with their children's schools will help to prove me wrong!

Happy ever after?

The journey towards a lesbian life is not easy. We have heard here just how difficult, painful and scary it can sometimes be. The loss of good friends, family upheaval, parental disapproval, social stigma and anxieties about the wellbeing of children are all difficult things to manage. Yet the overwhelming tone of these stories is not of self-pity or despair. Nor is it even one of heroic struggle in the face of great odds. It is joy, pure and simple. Joy at finding love, at experiencing new and extraordinary pleasures, at building a new kind of life and learning how to be a new kind of person.

The evidence of academics tells us that lesbian sex is the safest kind there is,[3] and that children brought up in lesbian households turn out at least as well (some suggest, better) than those from 'normal' families.[4] Psychologists have found that lesbians are likely to score better than non-lesbian women on indicators of psychological health such as self-esteem.[5] Sociologists suggest that lesbian relationships offer women more support for their career aspirations as well as their emotional needs.[6] Some studies even suggest we have fewer problems with the menopause than our non-lesbian sisters![7]

To this impressive list of academic endorsements must be added the experiences of the women whose stories have been told here. Of course, lesbianism is no magic solution to a woman's problems. Lesbian relationships can be painful and complicated, and hurt when they go wrong or end. The lesbian community, necessary though it is, can be a mixed blessing! Nor should we overlook or underplay the difficulties of being a lesbian in a world that still marginalises us at best; the consequences of homophobia are very real. Nevertheless, the business of lesbian life can be nothing short of life-enhancing.

Not every ending is happy: Margaret's story

I interviewed Margaret in a quiet café in London. Articulate and thoughtful, she has spent much time and energy reading voraciously to try to understand her attraction to women. Married to a man she respects and clearly feels affection for, she has not felt able to lay claim to a lesbian identity and her life has offered precious few opportunities to act on her feelings. Her story reminds us that, until very recently, living a lesbian life was an option open only to a tough and lucky few. It also warns us against trying to oversimplify the complicated experiences included in the word 'lesbian'. As she told me her story, somehow managing to speak without anger or self-pity, I wondered how many other women could tell similar stories. How many women have never had the simple freedom, which some of us take so much for granted, to be able to make any space in their lives for their yearning and desire?

*

It is difficult to know what to call myself. I hesitate to use the word 'bisexual', because that does rather imply that one might sleep around in any direction tomorrow, and in fact I have led an almost completely faithful sexual life with my husband since marrying in 1966. But I think I have very strong lesbian tendencies and, in spite of the fact that I pay tribute to a wonderful husband and all that, I don't feel that I would want to have another one! Should he die tomorrow my tendency would be to look for a similar type of long relationship with a woman.

I suppose you would say, why on earth did you marry him in the first place? Well, things were very different in the late 1950s and early 60s. If you had desperate 'crushes' on any females, this was described as immaturity and as something you would grow out of. I was also very much aware that I would like to be a mother and have children.

I grew up at a time when you had this ridiculous thing that little girls wore quite short dresses and yet there was a great thing about, no, you must *never* show your knickers. If they really wanted modesty we would have worn trousers or shalwar kameez or something similar. They didn't really want you to be safe from ever showing your knickers, they wanted to put the fear of god into you about it, so you had to keep your knees together. I remember being very aware of this, and very much aware that boys had freedom of movement and that trousers were wonderful!

I went to a girls' high school, and it was still in the age (which I suspect has gone now) when it was quite normal for little girls to have crushes on prefects and staff. I feel that disappeared with the 60s and 70s. I'm not saying it wouldn't happen, I'm just saying there wouldn't be words for it perhaps, all those different terms, the 'pash' and the 'crush', which were different in every school, I think! I remember them announcing that there would be a school dance and boys would be invited from the grammar school across the road. I remember feeling, oh, I don't want to go, then!

It was quite strange that I did manage to get married, because I never really showed much interest in men. I think my lack of interest in men is pretty obvious to them. Even men can notice that! I'm not going to kick them in the balls or anything, I am just fairly off hand. My husband was very persistent and had to ask several times until I finally decided that I would. But I am afraid to say – and I haven't admitted this *ever* out loud before – my main concern on my wedding day was whether a particular woman would show up at the wedding.

I was aware that I was not in love with my husband. I thought, and [from my reading I knew] that this had happened several times before to many others, that I would probably grow into the situation of being married. I haven't been a wonderful wife, but I don't think I've been that bad, actually. I did have one brief lesbian affair, which I'm not very happy about in retrospect.

This, I think, came about at a time when somebody I knew was arrested in a public loo. It made me think about homosexuality for the first time as something that ordinary people who you met in the street might be, and not some sort of monster. So I began to look back, I suppose, to reinterpret things that before had looked like immaturity. I thought, but I'm still feeling like that sometimes about some women at the age of 40! This is ridiculous, I'm not just immature. I haven't grown out of it and I don't seem to be likely to.

Having said that, these 'pashes' that I had were for women who were one hundred percent heterosexual and not the slightest bit interested. I do not cherish the illusion that, had I not married, I would have been perfectly happy and living in a rose-covered cottage with some nice lady somewhere. I think it's quite likely that I would have been a crabbed old miserable spinster with three dogs. So I'm not sorry for myself, let's say that.

My marriage? I feel we did a fairly good job. We have two children, grown up now, who are reasonably brought up, fairly well balanced. We lead somewhat separate lives in the sense that he has his hobbies and I have mine, so it's not like either of us is demanding anything terribly close. The sexual side works. I did for a while feel very sorry for myself about that, I didn't really want it very much. When I had this affair, I'd been twenty years married, so adjusting in that direction was perhaps more problematic than I would have thought.

There was a feeling of "I wish I could go back to 1960-something and know then what I know now." By then it was all just a bit late to create that upheaval. I still had children who were fairly young. I knew women who were doing that, and I moved in lesbian circles a little bit for a while and then – I don't know – it sort of faded out and became academic and bookish, rather from the sidelines looking in.

I turned it into an intellectual problem, as much as anything. Why is this one like this, why are they like that? It's one of those insoluble problems that one just solves, somehow. A reasonably stable human being can adjust amazingly to almost anything.

I do develop massive crushes on women. They usually last two or three years, I'm not slow to give up on them. It is painful. I just manage to have a private and a public life. I mean, a very much private inner life which, of course, is absolutely full of fantasy. I cannot remember a time when, if I had nothing else to do, I wasn't dreaming about women. Just walking up the road from the station! I suppose the last crush was around ten years ago and I'm always rather dreading the next one. It's been quite a long time, though, so maybe, whatever psychological forces are doing this, maybe they sort of wind down gradually with all the other things that wind down with age.

When my affair ended I continued to go to lesbian events, things like Kenric, perhaps in the hope of meeting somebody else. Then I became more realistic and thought, I'm sure there are plenty of women, so who on earth wants to get involved with a woman who isn't really wanting to leave her husband? I made that original contact – with the woman I had the affair with – from a contact ad in *Spare Rib*. I have always been quite feminist.

I suppose a lot of people must have described that sense of suddenly looking at your life, turning everything round and realising what it all means. A little bit like you've been holding a map upside down, and not understanding why you can't see the church that is supposed to be there; why don't the feelings match what they are supposed to have been? Then, suddenly, it's as if you have turned it around and, with the new angle, everything looks as if it is in the right place. For me, it was reading anthropology, and how the women carry all the burdens while the men saunter along with their bows and arrows pretending that they are going to hunt something.

So I feel two women in a relationship can probably get rid of a lot of the hassle that comes with trying to educate men in the fact that you are actually a human being.

There are regrets, yes, but I would feel different sorts of regret and probably guilt if my feelings had been reciprocated by women who were themselves married and had children. I don't think I would have been tough-minded enough to break up two marriages and wreck the lives of three or four children. I think I would have given myself a very hard time. Probably, relationships that started that way wouldn't have lasted anyway. Then you might be alone three years later, and what have you done all that for? I didn't have enough faith that any alternative would actually be better.

Notes

1. See: Barbee Cassingham & Sally O'Neil (eds), *And Then I Met This Woman: Previously married women's journeys into lesbian relationships*, Mother Courage Press, Racine, WI, 1993; Hall Carpenter Archives (eds), *Inventing Ourselves: Lesbian life stories*, Routledge, London, 1989; Sarah Holmes (ed), *Testimonies: A collection of lesbian coming-out stories*, Alyson, Boston, MA, 1988; Laura Markowe, *Redefining the Self: Coming out as a lesbian*, Polity, Cambridge, 1996; National Lesbian and Gay Survey (eds), *What a Lesbian Looks Like: Writings by lesbians on their lives and lifestyles*, Routledge, London, 1992; Suzanne Neild & Rosalind Pearson (eds), *Women Like Us*, The Women's Press, London, 1992; Edward Stein, *The Mismeasure of Desire: The science, theory and ethics of sexual orientation*, Oxford University Press, Oxford, 1999.
2. 'Able-bodied' is in quotation marks because few of us are without some kind of impairment and, for those who are severely unimpaired, this is at best a temporary state of being.
3. Lesley Doyal, *What Makes Women Sick*, Macmillan, London, 1995.
4. Fiona Tasker & Susan Golombok, *Growing Up in a Lesbian Family: Effects on child development*, Guildford Press, London, 1997.
5. Dominic Davies & Charles Neal (eds), *Pink Therapy: A therapist's guide to working with lesbians and gay men*, Open University Press, Buckingham, 1996.
6. Gillian Dunne, *Lesbian Lifestyles: Women's work and the politics of sexuality*, Macmillan, London, 1997.
7. Lee Lynch & Akia Woods (eds), *Off The Rag: Lesbians writing on menopause*, New Victoria, Norwich, VT, 1996.

Who They Were

The names (mostly pseudonyms) of the women who took part in this research, ages at the time of the interview and occupations.

Adie, 29, teacher
Ann, 37, swimming instructor
Anna, 35, joiner
April, 45, telesales representative
Barbara, 47, PR consultant
Barbara, 49, housewife/writer/voluntary worker
Carol, 55, retired postmistress
Catherine, 40, interior designer
Charis, 55, community care assistant
Charlotte, 30, unemployed youth worker
Claire, 24, postgraduate student
Claire, 39, chartered accountant
Dilly, 42, psychotherapist
Elizabeth, 45, local government training officer
Eve, 42, administration manager
Fiona, 35, artist
Florence, 44, senior psychiatric nurse
Gala, 45, university lecturer
George, 41, swimming instructor
Grace, 47, senior lecturer at university
Hannah, 26, PhD student
Helen, 36, therapist
Hilary, 37, theology lecturer
Jade, 49, research fellow
Jane, 53, foster carer
Janine, 31, broker
Jennie, 29, PhD student and motorcyclist
Jenny, 48, travel agent
Jill, 51, secretary

Jodie, 41, university security/porter
Jodie, 50, teacher/therapist
Julie, 35, community psychiatric nurse
Karen, 23, student
Karla, 26, performing arts student
Kate, 26, student midwife
Katie, 23, nurse/library assistant/student
Katie, 26, chiropodist
Kaz, 34, mother
Kerry, 32, sales manager
Kerry, 34, theatre designer
Kitt, 44, unemployed counsellor
Lee, 32, youth worker
Len, 38, psychiatric nurse
Lenna, 29, camera assitant/writer
Lesley, 30, mother of five
Lily, 45, voluntary sector co-ordinator
Liz, 42, administrator
Louise, 32, tax inspector
Louise, 33, journalist
Louise, 38, teacher
Margaret, 46, staff nurse
Margaret, 55, violin teacher
Marie, 28, assistant manager in a posh shop
Maureen, 34, civil servant
May, 39, library assistant, catering assistant
Michelle, 22, receptionist and law student
Michelle, 30, student of office technology
Nicky, 37, social worker
Nicky, 38, Women's Aid volunteer/parent assistant/OU student
Paula, 40, freelance trainer
Pippa, 49, watercolourist, living on benefit
Robbie, 48, university teaching fellow/adult education teacher
Ruth, 58, writer/teacher
Sally, 46, teacher
Sarah, 24, assistant facilities manager, DSS office
Sue, 44, retail pharmacist
Sue, 45, student and mother
Sue, 50, trainer in voluntary sector
Suzanne, 37, mother and gay switchboard volunteer
Theresa, 35, business studies student
Tina, 43, sales manager
Toni, 23, programmer
Vikki, 45, clinical trials packaging team leader
Virginia, 44, university lecturer
Zara, 39, SRN in neonatal intensive care

Resources

This section is designed to offer some signposts for women who are learning how to live as lesbians, and for those close to them whose lives are also touched and/or who want to offer support.

I have included books and contact details for useful organisations. Of course, this section could easily have turned into another book, but I have tried to keep it short and include only a few key resources. However, once you dip a toe in, you will find that one resource leads on to many more. Helplines will be able to point you in the direction of all sorts of groups, events and local networks, and most of the books listed here include their own bibliographies and suggestions for further reading. In short, this may not be a degree in lesbian living, but it is certainly an 'A' level!

First port of call

Your first port of call is likely to be one of the lesbian and gay switchboards that cover most of the country. Try ringing the London switchboard first, which has national coverage, but be aware that it may take a long time to get through – they are busy! If you are able to locate your local switchboard or lesbian line, phone them first. If not, the national switchboard should be able to give you a local contact number. You could also try looking up 'Friend' in the phone book. National Friend is an umbrella organisation that supports local lesbian and gay helplines. You will also find up-to-date information about these and other groups in the directory section of *Diva*. If your local bookshop doesn't stock *Diva* (try Tesco's and WH Smith before you give up!), ring them direct on: 020 8340 8644 (mail order) or 020 8348 9967 (subscriptions).

London Lesbian and Gay Switchboard 020 7837 7324
National information and support, 24 hours.
National Friend 0121 684 1261
London Friend 020 7833 1674
Women's line, Tues & Thurs evenings: 020 7837 2782
Kenric 01622 741213
Nationwide social organisation for lesbians of all ages.
Black Lesbian and Gay Centre 020 7620 3885
Helpline Tues & Thurs, 11 am–5.30 pm.
Brothers and Sisters Club (for deaf lesbians and gay men)
109 Kessock Close, Ferry Lane Estate, London N17.
REGARD 020 7738 6191
BM Regard, London WC1N 3XX. Email: regard@dircon.couk
National organisation for lesbians and gay men with disabilities.
Stonewall 020 7881 9440
Support and political lobbying, has a parenting group, an immigration service and a housing action group.
LAGER 020 7704 8066
Helpline: Mon–Fri, 12 noon–4 pm.
Confidential and free legal advice and support for all lesbians experiencing employment difficulties.

Other organisations

Parenting and families
Families and Friends of Lesbians and Gays 01454 852 418
Helpline and support network for parents coming to terms with their children's sexuality; also does campaigning work. FFLAG, PO Box No. 84, Exeter EX4 4AN. Website: www.fflag.org.uk Email: info@fflag.org.uk

Pink Parents 0117 904 4500
Helpline: 0117 377 5794
Helpline Thursday 7–10 pm. Email: enquiries@pinkparents.uk.com Website: www.pinkparents.org.uk Support and info, may be able to put you in touch with support in your area, lobbies for legal change.
Rights of Women 020 7251 6577
52–54 Featherstone Street, London EC1Y 8RT. Email: info@row.org.uk Offers free confidential legal advice to women on all aspects of family law, including lesbian parenting.

Religion and spirituality
Evangelical Fellowship (L&G Christians) 01276 24893
Gay and Lesbian Humanist Association 01926 858450
34 Spring Lane, Kenilworth CV8 2HB. Email: GALHA@bigfoot.com
Jewish Gay and Lesbian Group 020 8922 5214
BM JGLG, London WC1N 3XX.
Lesbian and Gay Christian Movement 020 7739 1249
Oxford House, Derbyshire Street, London E2 6HG. Email: lgcm@aol.com
Muslim Group
Email: alfatiha.london@hotmail.com
Quaker Lesbian and Gay Fellowship
Ruth (D), 46 The Avenue, Harrogate HG1 4QD.
Email: qlgfcontact@btclick.com
QUEST (Lesbian and Gay Catholic Group) 020 7792 0234
GLB Catholics, BM Box 2585, London WC1N 3XX.

Books

Parenting
Griffin, Kate, & Mulholland, Lisa (eds), *Lesbian Motherhood in Europe*, Cassell, London, 1997. Useful to get an overview of the situation facing lesbian mothers in different countries.
Rafkin, Louise (ed), *Different Mothers: Sons and daughters of lesbians talk about their lives*, Cleis Press, San Francisco, 1990. Reassuring accounts

from children of all ages about the impact of their mothers' lesbianism.
Saffron, Lisa, *It's a Family Affair: The complete lesbian parenting book*, Diva Books, London, 2001. Lots of information about how to start a family if you are already a lesbian, but there is also helpful material about other aspects of lesbian parenting and a useful resource section.

Religion and spirituality

Doe, Bishop Michael, *Seeking the Truth in Love: The Church and homosexuality*, Darton, Longman & Todd, London, 2000. Supportive and fair-minded book by a Church of England bishop – useful ammo when dealing with C of E members.
Helminiak, Daniel, *What the Bible Really Says about Homosexuality*, Alamo Square Press San Francisco, 1994. Very useful overview and summary of the theological arguments.
Stuart, Elizabeth, *Daring to Speak Love's Name: A gay and lesbian prayer book*, Hamish Hamilton, London, 1992.

Identity and sexuality

Califia, Pat, *Sapphistry: The book of lesbian sexuality*, The Naiad Press, Tallahassee, FL, 1988. There are many books on lesbian sex, and almost all of them are dire! Don't be tempted by glossy covers or colour pictures, this is the best available.
Clark, Don, *The New Loving Someone Gay*, Celestial Arts, Berkeley, CA, 1987. A Californian bestseller... British readers may find some of it squirm-inducing – and it holds to the 'born this way' line – but Clark is a therapist and gives useful suggestions on dealing with relatives, friends, etc., who are having problems accepting the new you.
Mason-John, Valerie, & Khambatta, Ann, *Lesbians Talk: Making black waves*, Scarlet Press, London, 1993. Essential information about racism in the lesbian community and how it feels to fight homophobia and racism. An important read, whatever the colour of your skin.
Trenchard, Lorraine, *Being Lesbian*, Gay Men's Press, London, 1989. Intended as a handbook for young lesbians just coming out, but has some useful things to say for older lesbians as well.
Wilton, Tamsin, *Good for You: A handbook on lesbian health and wellbeing*, Cassell, London, 1997. Perhaps I am biased, but this is the

only handbook on lesbian health written for British lesbians, and contains useful information on everything from sexual health to growing old as a lesbian.

History

Donoghue, Emma, *Passions Between Women: British lesbian culture 1668-1801*, Scarlet Press, London, 1993. Eye-opening revelations that make clear just how far back lesbian life in Britain can be traced.

Deitcher, David (ed), *Over the Rainbow: Lesbian and gay politics in America since Stonewall*, Boxtree/Channel Four Books, London, 1995. If you don't know what 'since Stonewall' means, you should read this book! The lesbian nation extends far beyond national boundaries, and lesbian culture in the US has been particularly influential.

Faderman, Lillian, *Surpassing the Love of Men: Romantic friendship and love between women from the Renaissance to the present*, The Women's Press, London, 1985. Groundbreaking study.

Hall Carpenter Archive Lesbian Oral History Group, *Inventing Ourselves: Lesbian life stories*, Routledge, London, 1989.

Hamer, Emily, *Britannia's Glory: A history of twentieth-century lesbians*, Cassell, London, 1996. An often amusing and non-academic collection of short biographies of British lesbians.

Healey, Emma, & Mason, Angela, *Stonewall 25: The making of the lesbian and gay community in Britain*, Virago, London, 1994. Everything you need to know about lesbian and gay politics in Britain, from the standpoint of a particular group of activists.

Neild, Suzanne, & Pearson, Rosalind, *Women Like Us*, The Women's Press, London, 1992. Heart-warming autobiographies of older lesbians.

Weiss, Andrea, *Paris was a Woman: Portraits from the Left Bank*, Pandora, London, 1995. Stylish accounts of the lives of some stylish lesbians, key figures in twentieth-century lesbian culture, with fascinating pictures.

Theory

Ruse, Michael, *Homosexuality: A philosophical inquiry*, Basil Blackwell, Oxford, 1988. Very academic, but contains a lot of fascinating facts. Ruse is trying to answer the question "Is homosexuality bad

sexuality?" and provides some useful ammunition en route.
Wilton, Tamsin, *Sexualities in Health and Social Care*, Open University Press, Buckingham, 2000. Primarily aimed at student nurses, but has useful summaries of the scientific theories and the religious arguments. Designed to be easy to understand!
Weeks, Jeffrey, *Sexuality*, Routledge, London, 2000. Small and concise, scholarly but approachable summary of the whole issue of sexuality.

Bookshops

Diva Mail Order
3 Broadbent Close, London N6 5GG. Tel: 0800 45 45 66 (international: +44 20 8340 8644). Website: www.divamailorder.com *Diva* magazine subscriptions, books, videos, etc.
Gay's The Word
66 Marchmont Street, London WC1N 1AB. Tel: 020 7278 7654. Website: www.gaystheword.co.uk Email: sales@gaystheword.co.uk Their ordering service is efficient and fast, and they can get most lesbian books and magazines for you.
Libertas!
42 Gillygate, York YO31 7EQ. Tel: 01904 625522. Website: www.libertas.co.uk Email: books@libertas.co.uk Bright bookshop and comprehensive mail-order service for lesbian books.
Silver Moon
3rd floor at Foyles, 113-119 Charing Cross Road, London WC2. Tel: 020 7437 5660. Website: www.silvermoonbookshop.co.uk Email: silvermoon@foyles.co.uk Famous women's bookshop with big lesbian section has moved to a revamped floor of Foyles.

US Organisations

If you don't know your local organisations, try one of these as a first port of call.

National toll-free lesbian and gay crisis line
run by the **Fund for Human Dignity** 1-800-221-7044

New York City Lesbian Switchboard (212) 741-2610
New York City Gay and Lesbian Switchboard (212) 777-1800
Dallas Lesbian Information Line (214) 528-2426
San Francisco Lesbian/Gay Switchboard (415) 431-1180

For young people
Insitute for the Protection
of Lesbian and Gay Youth (212) 473-1113
110 East 23 Street, 10th Floor, NYC 10010.

Sexual Minority Youth Assistance League
(Lesbian Youth Outreach Project) (202) 232-7506
1638 R Street, NW, #2, Washington, DC 20009.

Legal advice (including custody, employment, etc)
Lambda Legal Defense and Education Fund (212) 995-8585
666 Broadway, New York, NY 10012.

Websites
If you have internet access, things get a lot easier. You could start by logging on to **www.lesbian.org** – a website which acts as a virtual clearing house for a massive range of information useful to lesbians in the US and elsewhere.

If you have children (or would like to have children), try the lesbian mothers' website: **www.lesbian.org/lesbian-moms/**

OK... that's the map and survival kit, now off you go!

Also from Diva Books

It's a Family Affair:
The complete lesbian parenting book
Lisa Saffron

Indispensable help with the littlest big decision of your life

"Lisa Saffron has done a fantastic job, with every base covered, including adoption and fostering. Even if you're only just starting to think about kids, this book is a must" *Out in Greater Manchester*

"A comprehensive guide to becoming pregnant, giving birth, and bringing up children" Amazon

"Full of fascinating case studies with parents, children of lesbian parents, partners and surrogate fathers... dip in or read it cover to cover" *The List*

RRP £15 ISBN 1-873741-62-6

Girl2Girl:
The lives and loves of young lesbian and bisexual women
Edited by Norrina Rashid and Jane Hoy

Girls from across the UK write from the heart

"Gets my vote" TV's Trisha

"This anthology with its excellent resource section is a must for any young woman" *Time Out*

"Fun reading and a lifeline to the young and isolated, [a] very important book" *Gscene*

"Life-saving and inspiring" Skin, Skunk Anansie

RRP £8.95 ISBN 1-873741-45-6

Diva Books are available from bookshops including Silver Moon at Foyles and Libertas! or direct from Diva's mail order service: www.divamag.co.uk or freephone 0800 45 45 66 (international: +44 20 8340 8644).

When ordering direct, please add P&P (single item £1.75, two or more £3.45, all overseas £5) and quote the following codes: Unexpected Pleasures UNE723; It's a Family Affair ITS626; girl2girl DVB456.